The Jewish Woman and Her Home

NOTA KOSLOWSKY

The Jewish Woman and Her Home

BY

HYMAN E. GOLDIN

Illustrated by

NOTA KOSLOWSKY

HEBREW PUBLISHING CO.
NEW YORK

לזכר נשמת אבי מורי

ר׳ יהודה מנחם מנדיל ב״ר צבי ז״ל

לזכר נשמת אמי מורתי

מ׳ בתיה בת ר׳ דוד אריה ליב ז״ל

HEBREW PUBLISHING COMPANY
100 WATER STREET
BROOKLYN, NEW YORK 11201

L

ISBN 0-88482-427-6

TO THE JEWISH WOMAN

*"The Holy One, praised be He, has given to
woman more intelligence than to man."*
(NIDDAH 45b)

This book has been written to and for the
Jewish woman.   And yet not for her sake alone.
She, as mistress of the house, has an obligation
which extends beyond her own personal life.
In her hands, perhaps more than in any other,
lies the future of Jewish life.   She is responsible
for keeping alive the Jewish home, in which
all that is noble in Judaism is bred and fostered.
In her care are the children of Israel.

Many will read this book and perhaps become discouraged.   So many laws — so many
rules to remember!   But they must understand
that in Judaism there is something even more
essential than the laws themselves: the earnest
and honest endeavor to comply with the Law
of God.

The God of Israel neither asks nor expects
the impossible.   It is not how much one does
that counts, but the spirit in which it is done.

Say our Talmudic sages:

"Hakadosh barukh hu libba baee—"
The Holy One, praised be He, requires the heart.

[7]

In reading this book, each shall judge of her own ability to serve the Law. Each shall know in her own heart how honest and faithful is her effort to bring that Law into her home and into the hearts and minds of her children.

This book, however, must not be made an excuse for intolerance. It must not serve as a guide for condemnation of others. For the Talmud says:

"Yesh koneh olamo beshaah ahat—"
One moment suffices to acquire the future world.

It is therefore not within our province to judge our neighbors. The Almighty alone shall decide who shall be despised and who shall merit salvation.

If "THE JEWISH WOMAN AND HER HOME" will be used in this true Jewish spirit, it will not have been written in vain.

H. E. GOLDIN

Tishre, 5702 (October, 1941)

CONTENTS

CHAPTER ONE

THE JEWISH PEOPLE

CHAPTER TWO

MORAL LAWS — SOCIAL CONDUCT

CONTENTS

CHAPTER THREE

THE JEWISH HOME

CHAPTER FOUR

SABBATH (THE JEWISH DAY OF REST)

[10]

CONTENTS

CHAPTER FIVE

THE THREE PILGRIM FESTIVALS:
PASSOVER, SHABUOT, AND SUKKOT

[11]

CONTENTS

CHAPTER SIX

THE HIGH HOLY DAYS
(ROSH HASHANAH AND YOM KIPPUR)

CONTENTS

CHAPTER SEVEN

THE MINOR FESTIVALS

CONTENTS

CHAPTER EIGHT

THE FOUR FAST DAYS
(A SEASON OF NATIONAL MOURNING)

CHAPTER NINE

JEWISH FAMILY LIFE

CONTENTS

CHAPTER TEN

DEATH AND MOURNING

[15]

CONTENTS

CHAPTER ONE

THE JEWISH PEOPLE

"Whither thou goest, I will go; thy people shall be my people, and thy God my God."

(RUTH II, 16)

CHAPTER ONE

THE JEWISH PEOPLE

THE JEWISH WOMAN These are trying days for the Jewish people. Scattered in many lands, they are shunned, persecuted, and at best tolerated. But this very persecution is our national pride. The Jews are the noble martyrs of barbaric intolerance, and the disgrace is that of the tormentor and not of the tormented.

Now, especially, is it necessary that Jewish women understand this. Their men harried by economic needs have neglected their traditions. They have forgotten the lofty ideals for which the Jews have suffered throughout the ages.

It is therefore the woman's responsibility to fill that gap in Jewish life, to provide her home with that Jewish spirit which is too often lacking in most of our homes. And if she will plead incompetence and ignorance, I will say to her: "Look to your great and glorious past."

No other nation of the world owes so much of its cultural heritage to its women as ours.

[19]

At a time when other nations barbarously enslaved their women, considering them as chattel, the Jewish woman was already ranked among our poets, judges, prophets and great leaders of thought.

Let us open the pages of our great history so that we may understand the noble heritage of Jewish womanhood, and the role which you —our women of today—must once again prepare to take in the molding of the Jewish home.

THE ORIGIN OF THE JEWISH PEOPLE The origin of the Jews as a people differs from that of all other peoples of the earth. Abraham, traditional ancestor and founder of our religion, unlike other founders of nations, established a people not by means of conquests and bloodshed, but by a principle: the belief in the existence of one invisible power, GOD.

Abraham himself sprang from an old Chaldean family that dwelt in a land north of the Euphrates and thereafter migrated to Phoenicia, a land south of the Euphrates, later known as Canaan or Palestine. In this land, according to tradition, Abraham founded the tribe of the Hebrews. He rejected the religion of his pagan forebears, and preached the doctrine of the existence of only one God in heaven.

THE JEWISH RELIGION Once this Hebrew tribe accepted the premise of the existence of one single Power that controls the destinies of the universe, it gradually developed a religion befitting that divine Unity. Clearly, a God who is without body or bodily substance, cannot tolerate immorality, bloodshed and hatred. A divine unity, said the Hebrews, demands a united humanity without prejudices and hatred.

According to the accepted tradition, the basis of the Jewish religion was the Ten Commandments, delivered to the Jews on Mount Sinai by their God through the immortal teacher and prophet Moses, shortly after their departure from Egypt. The principles contained in these Ten Commandments were incorporated in the Five Books of Moses. These books record the laws of God as given to Moses by the Almighty for the benefit of the Jewish people. The cardinal principle of the Jewish religion is the golden rule laid down in the Holy Scriptures: "Love thy neighbor as thyself," or as paraphrased in later years by the great teacher and sage Hillel the Elder: "Whatever is hateful to thee, do not do unto others."

THE JEWISH HOMELAND For centuries the Jewish people lived and thrived in their land, now known as Palestine, where they observed the Law of God and went through various stages of spiritual and physical development. They were governed by judges and kings who waged wars and made conquests.

But governments and conquests, like all other material things, are not of an everlasting nature. Might is destroyed in time by another might. The indestructible things that the Jewish people did produce and develop in their homeland were the lofty ideals of their prophets. The prophecies and teachings of these prophets of God stand out as an eternal monument of Jewish spiritual development. The vicious brutal forces that have since arisen in the world have not been able to shatter that great monument.

The Jewish homeland, Eretz Yisrael, which produced these holy prophets, was therefore considered sacred, a holy spot chosen by the Almighty for the purpose of propounding His teachings. The Jews believed that this Holy Land had been singled out by God as a place of holiness, morality, and purity. Should its inhabitants become unworthy of occupying this holy soil, the Almighty would then drive them from the land.

The Jewish homeland was many times invaded by foreign conquerors. The Jewish people, on every occasion, defended themselves bravely. But in spite of their heroic sacrifices, their numbers were not great enough to withstand the persistent attacks, and they were finally compelled to leave their Holy Land and wander about as strangers in foreign lands.

For almost nineteen centuries the Jewish people have been estranged from their homeland. Yet, during all these long years, they have never given up the hope of returning to their fatherland. Morning, afternoon, and evening they have prayed to God for the restoration of their national freedom and the repossession of their land. They have never given up their nationalism, have never renounced their religion, and have never relaxed in their devotion to their God.

NATIONALISM The Jew was always proud of his people, proud that they were the first among nations to introduce morality, one God, tolerance, and peace. While all other nations of the world dreamt of conquests, of shedding blood, and of subjugating other peoples, the Jew dreamt of a world of peace and justice, love and tolerance.

This national pride was shared by Jewish men and women alike. The Jewish woman was proud of her people, and in times of need rose to leadership in the defense of her nation.

Several thousand years ago, when the Jews lived in Canaan under the ancient tribal system, they were often attacked and harassed by their savage neighbors. Because they lacked unified strength, they were sometimes forced to give up some of their towns to their enemies. It was at this time that the northern tribes of Israel were being terrorized by Jabin a Canaanite king, and by his general, Sisera, who commanded a large army heavily equipped with chariots of iron. Many inhabitants had to flee their homes and seek refuge in the land occupied by the tribe of Ephraim.

In the mountains of Ephraim lived a woman named Deborah who was endowed with a spirit of prophecy and poetry. People often sought her advice and judgment, and from her seat under the shade of a palm-tree, Deborah would teach the people to walk in the ways of God.

It was to her that the refugees from the north came. They told her of the terrible condition of their brethren, and their sufferings at the hands of the cruel Sisera. The gentle poetic soul of Deborah suddenly turned into that of a stern, heroic warrior. She called upon her people to unite and rise up against the enemy; summoning Barak, a warrior from the tribe of Naphtali, she bade him give battle to the invaders. Barak said to the prophetess: "If you will go with me, then I will go; but if you will not go with me, I will not go."

"I will surely go with you," replied the brave prophetess; "but the journey you take shall not be for your honor; for the Lord will give Sisera over into the hands of a woman."

The most valiant men from the tribes joined the army to wage war against Sisera, under the leadership of Deborah and Barak. When the formidable Sisera was informed that the Israelites had prepared for war, he set out against them with all his mounted soldiers. The two armies met in battle by the river Kishon, near Mount Tabor. Sisera's troops, unable to withstand the powerful attack of Barak's army, were utterly defeated. Sisera himself was forced to abandon his chariot and flee for his life. He fled into the tent of Jael, the wife of Haber, a member of the Kenite tribe which was on friendly terms with Israel. As soon as Sisera fell soundly asleep, Jael pulled one of the sharp tentpoles out of the ground, and drove it with a hammer into his temple, killing him instantly.

This great victory was commemorated by the prophetess in a beautiful war-poem, "The Song of Deborah," the first ever recorded in the annals of civilization.

ZIONISM In the last few decades, the Jewish dream of regaining Palestine, began to become a reality. By slow and almost insignificant degrees, young Jewish men and women are patiently rebuilding their homeland with their sweat and blood, never tiring, never yielding.

The Jewish women, shoulder to shoulder with the men, share the burden of rebuilding the Holy Land. Many young women, especially those from European countries, leave their homes and their native lands to settle in Palestine and rebuild it as a Jewish homeland. In every Jewish community in the world, the Jewish women who cannot migrate to Palestine are actively engaged in raising funds with which to purchase land in Palestine, helping young Jewish pioneers to settle there.

The organization, known as *Hadassah,* was established and is maintained by Jewish women all over the world. This organization supports and maintains hospitals, schools, and other charitable institutions in Palestine. Hadassah Chapters are being established in every sizeable Jewish community, especially in the United States of America and Canada.

Thus the spirit of the prophetess Deborah has continued to live through the dark sad history of the martyr people, the Jews. They combat their enemies with silent suffering and heroic endurance—by being kind and forgiving to their tormentors.

CHAPTER TWO

MORAL LAWS — SOCIAL CONDUCT

"Whatever way one desires to go, one is led."

(MAKKOT 10b)

שרה בת טובים

CHAPTER TWO

MORAL LAWS—SOCIAL CONDUCT

STUDY OF THE LAW There is a common misconception among our people that a Jewish woman is not obliged to study the Law of God. It is true that she need not study the vast Jewish religious literature merely for the sake of study, as is the duty of every Jewish man. But she is duty-bound to become thoroughly acquainted with all the laws and regulations which she must observe.

THE BELIEF IN ONE GOD The primary duty of every Jew is to believe in the existence of ONE GOD in heaven, the Creator of all existing things, who guides the destinies of mankind. This basic principle is contained in the first and the second of the Ten Commandments.

The mere belief in God and His unity, however, does not suffice. Our great sages teach us that the Jewish religion is founded not on mere belief but on actions and deeds. It is therefore the duty of every Jew to follow the ways of the Almighty and to adopt His attributes by being forbearing, kind, and merciful.

[31]

Idol-worshipers who believe in a multiplicity of powers can scarcely believe in the unity of mankind and in a world where peace and tolerance reign. Only believers in a unified divinity strive to achieve the unification of peoples and races by peaceful methods. It was because the Jew believed in an undivided Divine Power that he developed the prophetic ideal of a millenium of an undivided humanity, of universal peace and happiness, of the abolition of war and hatred among peoples.

"THE GOLDEN RULE" "And thou shalt love thy neighbor as thyself," is the Almighty's express command. It is the opinion of the great leaders of Jewish thought that this principle forms the basis of all Jewish laws.

It is recorded in the Talmud that in the first century B. C. E., a heathen, anxious to embrace Judaism, came to the great sage and scholar Hillel the Elder who was then President of the Jerusalem Supreme Court, the Sanhedren. The heathen said to the sage: "Teach me your whole Law while I stand on one leg."

In reply the sage laid down the golden rule: "Whatever is hateful to thee, do not do unto others. This," he added, "is the basis of the entire Jewish Law, while the rest is a mere commentary thereon. **Go and complete its study.**"

CHARITY "Thou shalt open thy hand wide unto him (the poor and the needy) . . . and thy heart shall not be grieved when thou givest unto him, because for this thing the Lord thy God shall bless thee in all thy works." These are the words of the Lord our God. And our sages, in interpreting this biblical passage, maintain that, in accordance with God's promise, the giving of charity does not impoverish the donor, but on the contrary enriches him. The Lord, they say, will surely bless the deeds of one who has pity on the poor. The sages further contend that the merit of giving charity is so great in the sight of the Lord God that as a reward for this the donor will be protected from all kinds of misfortune; he will be saved even from the very clutches of death.

The following story is one of many in the Talmud concerning charity:

The great Talmudic sage Rabbi Akiba ben Joseph was a sad father, for the astrologers had foretold that on the eve of her wedding, his daughter would die of the bite of a poisonous snake. However, he kept this knowledge to himself, and with anxious heart awaited his daughter's marriage.

The wedding ceremony passed most happily for all guests, but the heart of the unfortunate father was sad. The next morning, Rabbi Akiba hastened to his daughter's room to quiet the forebodings of a sleepless night. One can well imagine his delight and amazement when he saw his daughter not only alive but holding in her hand a large hair-pin thrust through the head of a poisonous snake. She explained to her father, that on retiring the previous night, she had removed this pin from her hair and stuck it in the wall for safe keeping. In the morning she had found the snake impaled on it.

The father now told his daughter all he had foreseen, and added: "Pray daughter, what charitable deed have you recently done to have deserved such a miracle?"

The daughter thought a moment and then anwsered: "Last night, at my wedding feast, I noticed a poor, old, hungry man standing alone near the door. He dared not enter the house because of his shabby clothes, and the servants were too busy to pay any attention to him. I then took the portion set before me, carried it over to the old man and made him welcome."

"Now I see the truth of the saying, 'Charity saves from death,' " exclaimed Rabbi Akiba joyfully, and he went immediately to the college to impress this lesson upon his numerous disciples.

There is, too, the example of our pious mother Sarah who in a world of ignorance and inhumanity was kind and helpful to the poor and needy. Sarah, herself wealthy and the wife of the honored 'godly prince,' cast aside all pride and station of life and daily sat at the entrance to her large tent in which there were always tables set with food and cold drink, and would invite weary travelers to enter and refresh themselves.

But no matter how virtuous the giving of charity may be, a married woman is subject to some restraint in practicing it. If she is dependent entirely upon her husband, having no income of her own, she is not allowed by the Jewish law to donate large sums of money to charity without her husband's knowledge and consent, unless she is certain that he would not object to it. She may give a small donation because it is presumed that her husband would consent. If, however, she is certain that her husband would object even to this, she may not do so. Under no circumstances should a married woman donate any sum of money to charity against her husband's will, because it would be considered theft for the purpose of giving charity, which is strictly forbidden in Jewish law.

If a woman has a wealthy husband, and she desires to assist her poor relatives, she is permitted by law to do so to any extent she pleases without obtaining her husband's consent; neither does she have to bring it to his attention, because he has no right to prevent her from assisting her next of kin. Should her husband refuse to permit his wife to make such contributions, he would be compelled by a Rabbinical court of law to give his consent.

If a married woman has an income of her own, independent of her husband, she is no longer guided by any of the above rules of law, but she is obliged by the law of God to give charity to the poor in accordance with her means.

In donating money for charity no distinction must be shown. The poor of all nationalities and creeds must be equally provided for.

Should any one come to your door for help, you may not turn him away empty-handed. Give him whatever you can, even if all you can afford is a morsel of bread. If you are unable to give anything at all, at least do not abuse the man, but speak kind words to him and express regret at your inability to help him. The Lord God will then have pity on you and bless you that you may be able to help the poor according to the desire of your heart.

One must neither rebuke nor speak harshly to the poor, for their hearts are broken and their spirits downcast. Whosoever puts the poor to disgrace and ridicule will have to account for it. One must be like a parent to the poor and show them mercy by deeds as well as by words.

When giving alms to the poor, do so with your whole heart and with a kind smile. Even if one gives a thousand pieces of gold, but is unfriendly and downcast about it, the deed is without merit, for it is marred by the manner in which is it done. It is not how much but how well you give that counts in the sight of the Lord God.

One should not boast of one's good deeds, and especially while in the act of giving charity. Charity should be given with as little publicity as possible, unless it is needed to encourage others to donate. The very pious among Jews make their charitable contributions in such a way that they themselves are not aware to whom they are giving it, and the recipients do not know from whom they are receiving it.

The highest virtue in giving charity is attained by the person who comes to the aid of those who have not yet reached the stage of actual poverty. Such aid may be in the form of a substantial gift or a loan, or even employment by means of which the poor man is relieved of the necessity of asking for alms from his fellow men. Nothing can excel such benevolence. The noble men and women in Israel, therefore, who form Loan Societies to advance money, without charging any interest whatsoever, for such purposes, are sure to receive a blessing from our merciful Father in heaven.

So important was the fulfillment of this precept to our Talmudic sages, that they counted it among the ten precepts for the fulfillment of which "the fruit is reaped in this world, whilst the principal is laid up for him in the world to come."

CARING FOR THE SICK When our father Abraham was ill, the Almighty—Healer of the sick —descended from heaven to visit him. Our sages say that a Jew must follow the ways of the Almighty by adopting His attributes: just as He heals the sick, so must every Jew help in providing a cure for the sick. If a sick man is poor and helpless, it is our sacred duty to provide him with all necessities. It is our duty to visit a sick person whether he be rich or poor, so that we may ascertain his needs, pray for him, and give him the pleasure of our company. Extreme care, however, must be taken not to become troublesome to the invalid.

When talking to a sick person, judgment and tact must be used, so as neither to discourage him nor to give him false hopes of a speedy recovery, for if the invalid be given false hopes, he will abstain from praying for mercy from Heaven.

Visiting the sick is likewise included by our Talmudic sages in the ten precepts for the fulfillment of which "the fruit is reaped in this world, whilst the principal is laid up for him in the world to come."

TREATMENT OF ORPHANS AND WIDOWS The more a person is depressed, the more careful must we be in dealing with him. We must be extremely cautious in our dealings with orphans and widows lest we cause them annoyance or displeasure. We are bound to help them as much as we can.

Moreover the Almighty expressly said: "Ye shall not afflict any widow, or fatherless child. If thou afflict them in any wise—if they cry unto Me, I will surely hear their cry."

Men and women who are helping to maintain institutions for orphaned children and widows are sure to be rewarded by our merciful Father in heaven who is knowr as "The Father of Orphans and the Judge of Widows."

DOWERING A BRIDE One great precept generally overlooked or neglected by the Jews is the dowering of the bride. It is the duty of every Jew, man and woman, to give financial help ard moral support to the poor bride, so that she may lack nothing at her wedding and not be disgraced in the eyes of her friends and her bridegroom.

The fulfillment of this precept was likewise regarded very important to our Talmudic sages, and they incorporated it in the ten for which "the fruit is reaped in this world, whilst the principal is laid up for him in the world to come."

HOSPITALITY "It is more meritorious to receive strangers in your house than to receive the Divine Presence," is the verdict of our Talmudic sages. This principle our sages learned from our father Abraham who excused himself before the Almighty who had come down to visit him during his illness, and ran to welcome three strangers into his house.

You, as a Jewish woman, should follow the example of our pious mother Sarah in being hospitable. Sarah would always be busily engaged in baking bread and preparing food for poor, stranded and weary wayfarers. Be especially kind to strangers, for away from their homes and families their hearts are embittered and they are in need of encouragement and consolation. Make them feel that they are welcome at your home, and offer them food even if they do not ask for it, for often they are ashamed to admit that they are hungry.

Our Talmudic authorities tell us that the reward for hospitality is so great that this precept, too, is included in the ten for the fulfillment of which "the fruit is reaped in this world, whilst the principal is laid up for him in the world to come."

TREATMENT OF FOREIGNERS As far back as the time of our great law-giver Moses, the following great and humane rule had already been cut in stone and written on papyrus: "One statute and one law shall be for you and for the stranger that lives in your midst." No discrimination must be shown between citizen and non-citizen, Jew or non-Jew. All strangers must be treated alike and receive the same benefits of the Law of God.

The same Law forbids us to take advantage of foreigners. We are warned by the Almighty neither to deceive nor oppress the stranger living in the land. Our Lord God even commanded that we must love the stranger. And this is one of the great virtues every Jew, man or woman, must possess.

HONESTY Honesty is a virtue every Jew must strive for. So important was honesty considered in the sight of the Lord God that He even admonished us to avoid temptation. Thus, we are forbidden to have inaccurate weights or measures in our possession, lest we be tempted to use them selling merchandise.

Our wise Talmudic scholars add: "Let your *yes* be honest, and let your *no* likewise be hon-

est." Your word must never be broken.
Whether given in the affirmative or in the nega-
tive, your word must always be fulfilled to
the letter, be it even to your hurt.

Concerning honesty, the Talmud also states:
"Let your mouth and your heart always be
in harmony." Speak only what you believe in
your heart to be true.

**PIETY—
HUMILITY**
Jewish women can be proud of their
ancestors who, even in the remotest
past, had already achieved a high
stage of piety and humility.

Can one fully appreciate and understand
the humble, pious Hannah, mother of the great
prophet Samuel? In a dark corner in the Temple
at Shiloh, she fervently prayed to the Almighty
that He grant her a male-child, so that she
would not die childless. No one was present
except the aged high priest Eli. Hannah's lips
moved only when she prayed, but her voice
was not heard. Never before had the high
priest seen any one pray without uttering a
sound. It was a new way of praying to the
Lord, silent devotion, introduced by the pious
Hannah. Eli thought that the woman was under
the influence of wine, and reproached her, say-

ing: "Oh you Jewish woman, how long will you be drunk? Put away your wine from you."

The pious Hannah became neither angry nor abusive, but bore the insult submissively, and gently replied to the aged priest: "No, my lord, I am a woman of sorrowful spirit; I have drunk neither wine nor strong drink, but I poured out my soul before the Lord God. Count not your handmaid for a wicked woman: for out of my great complaint and vexation have I spoken until now." Touched by the woman's humble spirit, and impressed with her gentle reply, Eli was remorseful, and said to Hannah: "Go in peace, and may the God of Israel grant your petition that you have asked of Him."

Hannah's petition was granted by the God of Israel, and the year after she gave birth to a male-child whom she named Samuel. After she weaned her son she brought him into the house of the Lord in Shiloh. She brought the child before Eli the high priest, and she said: "I am the woman that stood by you here, praying unto the Lord. For this child I prayed, and the Lord granted my petition which I asked of him; therefore I have lent him to the Lord; as long as he lives, he is lent to the Lord." The high priest was greatly impressed, and he took the child under his care in the Temple of God.

The pious mother before departing from Shiloh, expressed her feelings and her gratitude in a very beautiful poetic prayer, full of piety and trust in God. It was written almost three thousand years ago.

Multiply not exceeding proud talk;
Let no arrogance come out of your mouth;
For the Lord is a God of knowledge,
And by Him actions are weighed.

The bows of the mighty are broken,
And they that stumbled are girded with
    strength.
They that were full have hired themselves
    for bread;
And they that were hungry have ceased.

The Lord killeth and maketh alive;
He bringeth down to the grave, and
    bringeth up.
The Lord maketh poor, and maketh rich;
He bringeth low, He also lifteth up.

He will keep the feet of His holy ones,
But the wicked shall be put to silence in
    darkness;
For not by strength shall man prevail.

EMPLOYER AND EMPLOYEE Concerning the relations of employer and employee, Moses in the Holy Scriptures lays down the rule of law that it is a grave sin to rob a hired person of his wages or to cause undue delay in paying a hired man's wages.

A rule of law laid down by the Rabbis states that if a hired workman through negligence or otherwise spoils or destroys the article on which he has worked, it is the religious duty of the employer to waive his legal rights and release the workman from liability. There is an established principle in Talmudic law that charity and justice must be practiced to an even greater extent than is actually required by law.

The employee also has a duty towards his employer. When he is hired to do certain work, he must not cheat his employer by idling away his time. He must do all he is able to do, so that his wages may be justly earned.

HONORING FATHER AND MOTHER The fifth of the Ten Commandments given by God on Mount Sinai is: "Honor thy father and thy mother, that thy days may be long upon the land which the Lord thy God giveth thee."

According to the Talmudic sages, the fifth

commandment requires one to honor one's father and mother, to love them and to fear them, even as one must love and fear the Almighty. For honoring one's parents, the Almighty promised the reward, "that thy days may be long." The Almighty is anxious, so to speak, that one honor one's parents, because the parents and He are sharers in the creation, the former providing the material, and the Almighty the spiritual, part of the human being.

By fearing parents is meant that one should neither contradict them nor corroborate them in the presence of others; that one should not occupy the seats generally occupied by them in the house, even when they are away from home.

Children must cheerfully provide their parents with food, clothing and all else that they may need. The Talmudic authorities say that children who provide their parents with the finest luxuries, but do so with an ill grace, incur Divine punishment.

Parents must not be aroused from their sleep, even if because of their being asleep the children may lose much profit.

According to the Talmudic sages, parents must be honored even after their death. This can be accomplished by doing the biddings of the Lord God, by performing good deeds, and by following the path of virtue the parents have marked for their children.

If children put their father or mother to shame, even if only by looks or by words, they are included among those whom the Almighty has cursed, as it is written in the Holy Scriptures: "Cursed be he who lightly esteems his father or his mother."

The story of Jephtah's daughter as narrated in the Bible, tells how a Jewish woman, in devotion to her father, sacrificed herself because of her father's spoken word.

The Bible records that in the remote past, when Israel was ruled by local judges, a certain Jephtah, the leader of a robber band, was summoned by the elders of Gilead to become their leader and general in their contemplated war against the Ammonites. Jephtah agreed, and before joining the enemy in war, he made a rash vow: "If Thou, O Lord, wilt indeed deliver the children of Ammon into my hand, whatsoever cometh forth of the doors of my house to meet me upon my return, I will offer it up for a burnt-offering." The half civilized Jephtah was under the impression that our Father in heaven would be flattered by this vow and would in return grant him success in his war against the enemy.

Jephtah defeated the enemy completely, and triumphantly returned to his home-town. And who should be the first in coming out to greet the victorious warrior? His only daughter, in company of other youthful maidens, came out dancing and singing and playing.

"Alas, my daughter!" shouted the dejected father; "I have opened my mouth unto the Lord, and I cannot go back."

The young maiden understood the meaning of her father's fateful words. With firm resignation, without complaint, she consoled her unhappy father: "My father if you have opened your mouth to the Lord, do unto me whatsoever you have promised, since victory has been granted you."

Only a daughter of Israel, destined to bear oppression through the ages, could readily accept such resignation out of respect for her uncivilized father.

According to the Jewish law, children must honor and respect their step-mother during their father's life-time, and their step-father during their mother's life-time. However, it is highly proper that children honor their step-mother and their step-father even after the death of their parents.

The sin of disobeying the command of God regarding the honor due parents is very severe, and therefore our Rabbis laid down the law of conduct of parents so that their children might not be punished for their sake. They said that parents are forbidden to place an unbearable yoke upon their children; that they must not be too exacting with them in matters relating to the honor due them, so that their children might not thereby stumble into sin. The parents are obliged rather to overlook their children's shortcomings and to forgive them without reservation.

Parents are forbidden to chastise their grown-up children. And in this regard it does not actually depend upon the children's age but upon their nature. If there is reason to believe that the children will resent the punishment, and express such resentment either by word of mouth or by deed, it is absolutely forbidden to inflict corporal punishment upon them. They should merely be rebuked for their misdeeds by being shown why they were wrong. Our learned men say that parents who beat their grown-up children deserve to be excommunicated, because they are apt to bring sin and punishment upon their children.

RESPECT FOR ELDERS "Thou shalt rise before the hoary head, and honor the face of the old man, and fear thy God; I am the Lord." This admonition is embodied in the Law of God. It is the nature of the human being to belittle, and at times even to ridicule the old, and therefore our merciful Father in heaven ordered us to honor and respect the old for fear of His punishment.

According to the interpretation of the Talmudic sages, we must respect and honor a person advanced in years, even though he is not a scholar well versed in the Law. One learned in the Law of God of course, no matter what his age, must be respected and honored.

All needy persons must be provided for, but those engaged in the study of the Law of God and the learned men must be given special care and attention.

CRUELTY TO ANIMALS "The Lord is good to all, and His tender mercies are over all His works," sings the Psalmist. When, therefore, the Almighty bade us rest on the Sabbath, in the third of His Ten Commandments, He ordered us also to allow our animals to rest on that day. Again, He commanded us, that if we see an animal burdened with too heavy a load, even if the animal belongs to one whom we hate, it is our duty to have pity on the dumb animal and lighten its burden.

In this case, too, Jewish women have had an example set for them long ago by Rebecca that one must pity animals, even though it involves much toil and labor. The kind Rebecca was at a well drawing water for her home. Eliezer, the servant of Abraham, was near the well with his ten camels laden with riches. He had come there on a mission from his master to choose a wife for Abraham's son Isaac. He asked Rebecca for a little water to quench his thirst. Kind Rebecca not only gave him fresh water to drink, but also laboriously drew enough water to satisfy the thirst of the ten camels who had travelled through the hot desert without water.

The Law of God forbids the infliction of needless pain and suffering upon any living creature. Thus it is forbidden to set a bird on eggs that are not of her species; it is likewise forbidden to tie the legs of an animal or the wings of fowl in such manner as to inflict pain.

It is the duty of every person to relieve

any living creature of pain, whether it is ownerless or not.

According to one of our great Talmudic sages, we are obliged to feed our fowl and beasts before sitting down to our meals.

An interesting story is recorded in the Talmud to illustrate the importance of being kind to dumb animals.

Rabbi Judah ha-Nasi, the great Talmudic scholar who compiled and edited the Mishnah, was walking one day in the market-place when a young calf which was being led to slaughter hid its head underneath the Rabbi's mantle and lowed mournfully. "Go thee thy way," said the Rabbi, because for this purpose wert thou born." For this utterance, the Rabbi was punished with great bodily suffering for many years.

One day Rabbi Judah ha-Nasi noticed that his servant while sweeping the house was about to sweep out a litter of new-born kittens. The Rabbi interfered and said: "Let them be, for it is written, 'And His tender mercies are over all His works.' " It was then said in heaven: "Since he shows pity, he deserves to be pitied." From that time on the Rabbi was relieved of his affliction.

GOOD VIRTUES Our sages teach us, that to enjoy happiness in life, we should in every instance adopt the middle course, the happy mean, and not the extreme. It is improper to desire luxuries, or things that are not actually needed for a healthy existence. Unnecessary and lavish spending leads to dishonesty and crime. On the other hand, one must neither be shiftless nor be satisfied with less than one needs for sustenance. It is the Almighty's desire that we enjoy life and the bounties of nature in moderation.

One should not be too jocular and gay, nor too morose and melancholy; but should at all times be happy, friendly, amiable, satisfied and pleasant. The person who adopts the middle course in life is considered wise and pleasing in the sight of the Almighty.

Silence is a great virtue. Prattle and loose talk lead to foolishness and indiscretion, and should therefore be avoided. Speak only of matters appertaining to wisdom, learning, and the necessities of life. One of our great sages said: "He who desires life will find it in the tongue, and he who desires death will likewise find it in the tongue."

It is your duty to speak kindly to *every* person, but you must be especially careful to speak kindly to orphans, widows, and to all other persons in suffering or distress. Do not vex them even with words, because their souls are downcast and their spirits low.

Should you see anyone trying to commit a sin, it is your duty to convince him that he is doing wrong. If, however, you are certain that the sinner will pay no attention to you, then you are actually forbidden to rebuke him.

Every Jewish woman must know this great principle laid down by our wise men: Never conduct yourself in such manner as to arouse suspicion.

ENCHANTMENT AND SUPERSTITION

It is very unfortunate, indeed, to observe that many of our Jewish people, especially women, have fallen into the snare of idolatrous beliefs. Some Jewish women who are suffering physical pain unconsciously become idol-worshipers by turning to Christian Science for salvation, believing that this will relieve their suffering. Salvation can come only from our Father in heaven who is the Healer of all diseases. In Him alone must we believe, and if we look for help from any other source, we are guilty of the very serious sin of idol-worship. One cannot believe in Christian Science and be really a Jew at the same time.

The Lord our God commanded in His Law: "Neither shalt thou use enchantment nor observe times." Our sages explain that the term *enchantment* used in the Holy Bible includes all kinds of superstitious beliefs. Belief in superstition is absolutely forbidden because it savors of witchcraft and disbelief in God. You must not consult a wizard, a witch, or a soothsayer, or gypsies, or fortune-tellers, or cards, or tea-leaves, because by doing so you deny the Almighty's control over human destinies.

The prohibition against practicing enchantment also precludes the belief in omens which people are accustomed to read into certain things that happen to them. For instance, some people consider it ill-luck when bread drops from their mouth, or a cane falls from their hands, or when their sons call them from behind, or a raven croaks to them, or a deer or a black cat crosses their path, or when a fox passes on their right or a snake on their left, or when they are met empty-handed; some believe thirteen to be an unlucky number. Some consider it a good omen when met by one who is full-handed. All these superstitions must be rejected unconditionally by Jews.

One must not knock on a wooden object and say "knock on wood," in order to ward off the effects of an "evil eye." This, too, is a foolish superstition and is classed as enchantment.

The prohibition against *observing times,* according to the definition of our sages, forbids one to believe in horoscopes, to speak of one day or month or year as being lucky or unlucky for certain enterprises.

When asked to repay a certain loan, one must not say: "I pray you, leave me alone now, because it is early in the morning, and I do not wish to begin the day by making payments." Neither may one answer: "It is the close of the Sabbath and I do not wish to begin the week by making payments;" or, "It is the New Moon, and I do not wish to begin the new month by making payments." Any one using these or similar expressions is guilty of violating the command of the Almighty.

TALEBEARING—
SLANDER

"Thou shalt not go up and down as a talebearer among thy people," is the command of our Father in heaven. According to the definition of our Rabbis, this prohibition refers to the gossip monger; for instance, when one says: "Thus said so and so concerning so and so;"

or "I have heard such and such about him."
Even if the gossip be true and hurts no one,
it is a violation of the Law of God, and constitutes the crime of talebearing. The conse-
quences of talebearing are shown in the story of
Doeg and Edomite. Doeg told King Saul that
Ahimelech, the high priest, had given food and
a sword to David, who had run away to escape
Saul's fury. Doeg told the truth; and Ahimelech himself would have told the king what he
had done, because he had no intention of sinning
against Saul. Yet the talebearing of Doeg
caused the loss of many lives. King Saul in his
mad fury called for Ahimelech, the high priest,
and demanded an explanation of his deed. Although the high priest justly pleaded innocence,
Saul ordered that all priests living in the city
of Anatoth be punished with death.

Slander consists in purposely holding someone up to ridicule by the revelation of true facts.
For instance, one would be guilty of slander if
one said with malicious intent: "So and so has
done such and such a thing," or "I have heard
such and such about him," or "so and so were
that one's parents." Slander is a much graver
sin than talebearing, and our Rabbis say that
to the slanderer the words of the Psalmist apply:
"May the Lord cut off all the flattering lips, the

tongue that speaketh boastful things." In short, do not say anything about anybody, even if it be the truth, with the intention of holding him up to ridicule.

One may sometimes be guilty of the grave sin of slander, by simply insinuating that one knows something about any one which one does not wish to reveal, thus implying that the person referred to is of doubtful character.

If one maliciously invents untruths about a person, then one is guilty not only of the grave sin of slander but of defamation of character as well. According to our Talmudic authorities, a person guilty of the latter crime will have no share in the world to come.

One who listens to talebearing, slander, and defamation is considered by our sages even more guilty than the person telling it, because he encourages the sinner by listening.

NOT TO BE VINDICTIVE "Thou shalt take no vengeance," is another command of the Lord our God recorded in the Law of Moses. Vengeance is illustrated by the Rabbis as follows: You ask your neighbor to lend you a certain thing, and you are refused. The following day, your neighbor wishes to borrow something from you, and you say: "I will not lend it to you, because yesterday you refused to lend me what I had asked for." If you do not wish to violate the Law of God, then you must lend the thing to your neighbor with your whole heart and without having any grievance, entirely forgetting your neighbor's refusal.

"Thou shalt not bear a grudge," is the continuation of the above injunction, and it is illustrated in this way by our Rabbis: You ask your neighbor to lend you something, and you are refused. After some time your neighbor comes to borrow something from you, and you say: "Lo, I will lend the article to you, in spite of the fact that you refused me what I asked you for." To comply with God's law, you must make the loan wholeheartedly, and make no mention of your neighbor's past action.

In brief, do not be vindictive. If you will readily forgive them that have wronged you, your sins and wrongdoings will be forgiven by our Father in heaven.

WRONG DONE BY MEANS OF WORDS Be extremely careful not to hurt anybody's feelings by your words.

Do not say to your penitent neighbor: "Remember your former deeds."

Do not call anybody by an approbrious

nickname, even though everybody else calls him by that name, and he does not seem to mind it.

Never go out shopping and pricing articles when you have no intention of buying them.

Never ask any one to dine with you, when you know that your invitation will not be accepted.

Make no attempt to present any one with a gift, when you are certain that it will be refused.

Flattery is a vice that the Almighty shuns. Therefore praise no one whom you really do not wish to praise.

DECEPTION It is strictly forbidden by the Law of God to deceive anybody—Jew or non-Jew—by word or deed. This injunction applies not only to business dealings, but also to personal deceptions even though they be in jest.

It is especially sinful to mislead the innocent either by inducing them to commit a crime, or by putting hindrances or stumbling blocks in their way, or by falsely advising those who ask for counsel. Our merciful Father in heaven expressed the prohibition against such practices in the following injunction: "Before the blind, thou shalt not put a stumbling block."

NOT TO COVET The tenth of the Ten Commandments is: "Thou shalt not covet thy neighbor's house . . . nor anything that belongs to thy neighbor."

The violation of this moral law leads to the transgression of many other commandments. Covetuousness and jealousy lead to theft, adultery, murder and many other gross violations of God's Law. That is why this moral prohibition was given as a sort of summary to the Ten Commandments.

THEFT AND ROBBERY The right to possess property is sacred among the Jews, and therefore none may interfere with one's lawful and peaceful possession of such property.

The eighth of the Ten Commandments is: "Thou shalt not steal." According to the Talmudic sages, the eighth commandment prohibits not only the theft of tangible property and kidnaping, but also the stealing of one's honor, business, or reputation, and the stealing of one's mind by deception.

Neither the value of the article stolen nor the condition of the rightful owner may change the fact of the transgressor's guilt.

Jewish law strictly forbids stealing even though it be with the intention of returning the stolen article to its rightful owner. This is sometimes done as a practical joke or merely for the sake of annoying someone.

It is strictly forbidden to derive any benefit from another's property without the other's knowledge and consent, even if one is sure that the owner would not only not object but be pleased by such use of his property.

To make amends the thief must restore the stolen article to the owner. If the stolen article has been destroyed or altered, he must pay the owner as much as the article was worth at the time of the theft. If the person from whom the article was stolen is no longer alive, restitution must be made to his heirs.

It is a serious sin in Jewish law to buy stolen goods from a thief, because it encourages the commission of crime.

It is forbidden to derive any benefit from stolen articles as long as they remain in the thief's possession.

No charitable contributions may be accepted from a notorious thief whose property is presumed to have been acquired by theft and robbery.

INJURIES TO PERSONS One is forbidden to inflict bodily injury upon another. Our sages say that he who merely raises his hand with the intention of striking another is called *rasha* (wicked).

It is obligatory upon every Jew to do everything possible to save another from being hurt. If we cannot ourselves come to the rescue, it is our duty to engage others to do so.

It is a serious offense, in Jewish law, to be an informer (*moser* in Hebrew)—to surrender, by deed or word, the person or the property of another into the hands of the heathen. So grave was this crime considered by our Talmudic scholars that they ruled that an informer will have no share in the world to come. If, however, a man is betrayed and he has no chance of proving his innocence without informing against his betrayer, he is permitted to do so.

DAMAGE TO PROPERTY The Jewish law forbids one to damage another's property either directly or indirectly. In some cases, the law cannot force one who has caused such damage to make reparation. Nevertheless, the perpetrator of the act is guilty of transgressing a moral law in the sight of the Divine Court.

The wrong deed will not be forgiven by Heaven unless reparation is made, and unless the wronged party is conciliated.

One may not cause damage to another's property even if he does so with the express intention of making reparation.

Neither by deed nor word may one cause another to suffer loss. One guilty of such a transgression violates the Divine Law, and the guilt can be expiated only by conciliating the injured party.

One is not permitted, even on one's own premises, to do anything which may cause one's neighbor to sustain damage or be annoyed.

BEQUESTS Our learned Rabbis say that the Almighty takes no delight in one who bequeathes all his property to strangers, even though it be for charity. It is sinful to disinherit one's natural heirs. That one's natural heirs may not have behaved properly is immaterial.

One may not bequeathe a larger portion to one child than to another, even though one child may seem more worthy.

VICES Pride, even in the slightest degree, is an extreme vice in the eyes of our law-makers. Arrogance and pride lead to transgression and sin. Every Jew must be humble in spirit. Consider, therefore, every person to be better and greater than you are. Let all your words be uttered in a low gentle voice.

"Bear no hatred in thy heart against thy neighbor," is God's declared will. If anybody wrongs you, do not bear a silent hatred against him. Be outspoken; talk the matter over with him who wronged you, so that you may reach an understanding with him and forgive him.

Neither should you invoke the judgment of Heaven against him who has wronged you, nor pray that evil come upon him. Truly pious Jews should adopt the virtue of forgiving the wrong-doer without rebuking him. The Jewish woman who attains such virtue will be highly rewarded by Heaven.

Anger is a grave vice about which our Talmudic authorities say: "A person who becomes angry is considered as though he had served idols." Many follies and heinous crimes have been committed in moments of anger.

It is a sin to insult anyone, either by word or by deed. Our Rabbis tell us that public insult is considered as grave a crime as bloodshed, and one guilty of the crime will have no share in the world to come. Refrain therefore from calling anyone by an insulting name, or from narrating in a person's presence anything of which he feels ashamed.

Under no circumstances should you speak scornfully of anyone whether he be present or not. All form of mockery is forbidden in the Jewish law.

Telling untruths is hateful in the sight of the Lord our God who forbade it in the following words: "Ye shall not lie one to another."

Avoid flattery and hypocrisy.

The Talmudic teachers say that scorners, hypocrites and liars are not worthy of receiving the Divine Presence.

Cursing is a very ugly habit. Our sages say that God's blessing will not be bestowed on a house where curses are heard.

Quarreling should by all means be avoided, because it generally leads to hatred. It is therefore the duty of every Jewish woman to maintain peace and harmony at home. Never answer insult with insult or anger with anger; but forget and forgive. King Solomon advised: "A kind answer turneth wrath away."

Jealousy is a grave vice, for it leads to the violation of many laws causing unnecessary misery and suffering.

Swearing is strictly forbidden by Jewish law. Our Rabbis say that the third of the Ten

Commandments — "Thou shalt not take the name of the Lord thy God in vain"—not only warns us not to swear falsely, but also to abstain from taking an oath under any circumstances, even for the purpose of merely strengthening a statement. If, however, one does take an oath, one must abide by it.

The unnecessary mention of God's name, in such expressions as, "For God's sake," or, "By God," is likewise forbidden, for it leads to the abuse of the Divine Name.

THE JEWISH HOME

"And thou shalt know that peace is thy tabernacle;
and thou shalt visit thy habitation, and shalt miss
nothing."

(JOB v, 25).

CHAPTER THREE

THE JEWISH HOME

THE JEWISH HOME The home of the Jew must bear a distinctive character. The Jewish home must be made a sacred institution where all the laws pertaining to the home must be observed. Every home can thus be turned into a holy shrine where godliness prevails.

In the philosophy of the Jewish religion, holiness is not confined to any one class or to one special place. God is to be found not only in temples and synagogues, but everywhere, in whatever places are made holy by the deeds and thoughts of human beings. Our homes, too, are under the protection of the Almighty, if in them we so conduct ourselves as to invite His presence among us.

Godliness is not confined merely to those who are learned in the Law. If our thoughts are pure and our deeds worthy, we can attain God's mercy even when we are not ordained ministers of religion. Of course, it is our duty to study and listen to the teachings of learned men so that we may distinguish between right and wrong.

Speaking to the Jewish people, God said: "And ye shall be unto Me a kingdom of priests and a holy people." All Jews, then, are priests and holy if they follow His teachings: if they are god-fearing, merciful, kind, and peaceloving; if their homes have a Jewish atmosphere; if peace and harmony exist between husband and wife, parent and child; if in their homes God's words are heard and discussed; if sacred books are studied there. Then every member of the family is a priest unto God; the home is a shrine; and the table is an altar of God.

MEZUZAH Jewish women should know that their religion is unique in that it controls and regulates every phase of Jewish life. Its rules of conduct regulate our dealings with our fellow-men, our every-day actions, our mode of thinking, the conduct of our private lives and of our homes.

God commanded through Moses that His word must be written "upon the door-posts of thy house and upon thy gates." Our Talmudic sages interpreted this command to mean that the Law of God is not actually to be written on the door-posts, but that a *mezuzah* be fastened to them. The *mezuzah* is a small sheet of parchment upon which are inscribed by hand two paragraphs of the Law of God which are read by Jews in the *shema* prayer every morning and evening. These paragraphs begin with the words: "Shema yisrael, adonai elohenu, adonai ehad," meaning: "Hear, O Israel, the Lord our God, the Lord is one," and ending with: "And thou shalt write them (the laws) upon the door-posts of thy house and upon thy gates." On the reverse side of the parchment, the word *Shadai* (Almighty) is inscribed. This parchment is encased in a metal or wooden tube which is nailed to the door-post.

The *mezuzah* fastened to the door-post reminds us: (a) That those who occupy these premises believe that there is only one God in heaven and on earth; and (b), Of the presence of God in that home. And since our Father in heaven is always in our midst, our houses must always be godly, holy and peaceful, and we must abstain from doing any act which is evil in His sight. There must be no quarreling, no cursing, no hatred, and no slanderous talk. To constantly remind the inhabitants of the Jewish home of the presence of the *mezuzah* and its object, there has developed the beautiful custom of kissing the *mezuzah* upon entering and leaving the house, so that they may be god-fearing both at home and outside of it.

The *mezuzah* also had another object. Many, many times during the long bitter persecution of the Jew, he was compelled to leave his home and wander from place to place, begging for help. And to whom could the unfortunate Jew turn, if not to his fellow Jews? In his wanderings, the Jew would often go without shelter or food for days. How great was his joy then when at last he would find a house with a *mezuzah* fastened to its door— a house where he might be sure of welcome, food and rest. The *mezuzah* is therefore a symbol of hospitality and brotherly love.

LAWS CONCERNING THE MEZUZAH The Jewish woman, too, is obliged to fulfill the command to affix the *mezuzah* to the door-posts of her home. She must therefore become acquainted with the most important laws concerning the *mezuzah*.

The *mezuzah* must be affixed to every door of the house. If one occupies many rooms, and in every room there are many doors made for exit and entrance, one must affix the *mezuzah* to each one of these doors, even if only one of these doors is actually used.

An entrance without a door, or with a folding door, requires a *mezuzah,* but no benediction should be pronounced before affixing it.

A *mezuzah* should never be affixed to the door-post of a bath-room.

When placing the parchment in the case, it must be rolled in such manner that the first word *shema* is on the top. The case must be fastened to the door-post diagonally, having the top line containing the word *shema* toward the house, and the last line towards the outside. If the door-post is not wide enough, the *mezuzah* may be fastened to it perpendicularly. The *mezuzah* is not considered valid if it is merely suspended; it must be fastened with nails at top and bottom.

The *mezuzah* must be affixed within the upper third of the door-post. It must be on the right hand side as one enters, and on the outside. If by error it is affixed to the left hand side, it is invalid. It must then be removed and affixed to the right hand side, and the benediction must be repeated before refastening it. It is immaterial whether one is right-handed or left-handed, one must always be guided by the majority as to what is the right and what is the left.

Immediately before affixing the *mezuzah,* the following benediction is said:

בָּרוּךְ אַתָּה יְהוָֹה אֱלֹהֵינוּ, מֶלֶךְ הָעוֹלָם, אֲשֶׁר קִדְּשָׁנוּ בְּמִצְוֹתָיו, וְצִוָּנוּ לִקְבֹּעַ מְזוּזָה.

"Barukh attah adonai, elohenu melekh haolam, asher kidshanu bemitzvotav, vetzivanu likboa mezuzah."

"Praised be Thou, O Lord our God, King of the universe, who hast sanctified us by Thy commandments, and hast commanded us to affix the *mezuzah.*"

If several *mezuzot* are to be affixed at one time, the saying of one benediction before affixing the first *mezuzah* will suffice for all. If a *mezuzah* happens to fall off by itself from the door-post, the benediction must be repeated when it is affixed again.

WASHING THE HANDS IN THE MORNING Every human being when rising from his sleep in the morning is like a new-born creature so far as the worship of the Creator is concerned. Each should therefore prepare himself for such worship by purifying himself. He should wash his hands ritually by spilling water on them three times, even as the high priest used to do before beginning his service. A woman, who handles food, must exercise even greater care than a man in observing such ritual hand-washing in the morning.

While performing the ritual handwashing, no soap may be used; but soap may be used immediately thereafter.

The following benediction is said immediately after washing the hands and before drying them:

בָּרוּךְ אַתָּה יְהֹוָה אֱלֹהֵינוּ, מֶלֶךְ הָעוֹלָם, אֲשֶׁר קִדְּשָׁנוּ בְּמִצְוֹתָיו, וְצִוָּנוּ עַל נְטִילַת יָדַיִם.

"Barukh attah adonai, elohenu melekh, haolam, asher kidshanu bemitzvotav, vetzivanu al netilat yadaim."

"Praised be Thou, O Lord our God, King of the universe, who hast sanctified us by Thy commandments, and hast commanded us concerning the washing of the hands."

THE ARBA KANFOT By the command of the Almighty, through His prophet Moses, the Jews were ordered to wear *tzitzit* (fringes) attached to the four corners of a garment. The reason for wearing the *tzitzit* is given by the Almighty: "That you may look upon them and remember all the commandments of the Lord, and do them." The special garment with the four fringes attached to it, is known as *arba kanfot*. This ritual garment is "the Jewish coat-of-mail," as further told by the Almighty: "That ye seek not after your own heart and your own eyes." He who wears the *arba kanfot* will be able to ward off unworthy and immoral impulses; this garment will instill in the wearer an idealism and a determination to abide by the laws of God and abstain from doing evil.

You, Jewish mothers, can implant in the hearts of your children reverence and love for the Jewish ideals and traditions by explaining to them intelligently the religious meaning of this symbol. Inexpensively you can so mould the character of your children that when they grow up they will not prove to be a source of pain, grief, and shame to you.

For a very small sum of money you can supply your boys with an adequate supply of these religious garments which can be purchased at shops selling religious articles. Make them wear the *arba kanfot*, and explain its importance to them.

The *arba kanfot* is generally put on in the morning before reciting the morning prayers, while reciting the following benediction:

בָּרוּךְ אַתָּה יְהֹוָה אֱלֹהֵינוּ, מֶלֶךְ הָעוֹלָם, אֲשֶׁר קִדְּשָׁנוּ בְּמִצְוֹתָיו,
וְצִוָּנוּ עַל מִצְוַת צִיצִת.

"Barukh attah adonai, elohenu, melekh haolam, asher kidshanu bemitzvotav, vetzivanu al mitzvat tzitzit."

"Praised be Thou, O Lord our God, King of the universe, who hast sanctified us by Thy commandments, and hast commanded us concerning the precept of putting on a fringed garment."

Girls are exempt from wearing the fringed garment.

THE MEANING OF PRAYERS Even in the earliest days of the history of mankind, people sought to establish communion with deity, however crude their concept of deity might have been. Man has always expressed a yearning to communicate with his deity, to show him gratitude and pay him homage, and to speak to him of needs and fears.

During the existence of the Jewish commonwealth, the Jews adopted the method of sacrificing offerings to their God as a means of communicating with Him. On certain occasions, the Jews offered fervent prayers, in addition to bringing sacrifices.

With the destruction of the Temple, when sacrifices were no longer possible, the Jews adopted the method of prayer to establish communion with their God. Those prayers are seldom offered for individuals and their needs; they are mostly national in their character, calling for the restoration of Zion and the coming of the Messiah. Many prayers bear the character of universalism, praying for all peoples to recognize the existence of the true God in heaven, for universal peace, the cessation of hostilities, and brotherhood among men.

Prayer is a part of Jewish spiritual life, and woman as well as man must offer prayers to the Almighty, thereby acknowledging His sovereignty over the universe. By praying to him, we also acknowledge that in His hands are the destinies of all men, and nothing can be accomplished without His will.

It is not necessary that the Jewish woman utter many and lengthy prayers, or read everything written in the Prayer Books. It is enough to pray as pious Hannah prayed: silently, with heart and soul, and with full confidence and faith in Him to whom you are praying. Our Talmudic sages said: "It is better to pray little with devotion, than to pray much without devotion."

When praying to God, your mind as well as your body must be thoroughly clean; otherwise do not pray at all. Our great sages said: "Know you before whom you are standing to pray: before the supreme King of kings, the Holy One, praised be He."

It is the sacred duty of every Jewish mother to teach and train her children, sons and daughters, how to pray, morning and evening, in order that they may come nearer to God and to His teachings.

Morning Prayer for Children

"Praised be Thou, O Lord our God, Father of all, for letting me see this new day.

"Praised be Thou, O Lord our God, Father of all, for having given us a law of truth and for having implanted eternal life within us.

"The Torah which God gave through Moses is the heritage of the congregation of Jacob.

"Hear, O Israel, the Lord our God, the Lord is one.

"Blessed be His name, whose glorious kingdom is for ever and ever.

"You shall love the Lord your God, with all your heart, and with all your soul.

"And these words which I command you this day, shall be upon your heart. You shall

teach them to your children, and you shall speak
of them when you sit in your house, and when
you are on the road; when you lie down and
when you awake. And you shall bind them
as a sign upon your hand, and they shall be for
frontlets between your eyes. And you shall
write them upon the door-posts of your house
and upon your gates.

"O God, guard my tongue from evil, and
my lips from speaking falsehood.

"O Lord, help me to understand Thy teachings, and to be faithful to all my duties.

"Let my prayers be acceptable in Thy
sight, O Lord. Amen."

Evening Prayer for Children

"Praised be Thou, O Lord our God, Father
of all, for giving us the sweet rest of the night.

"In peace do I lay me down to sleep, and
may it be Thy will, O Lord, that I awake in
peace.

"Hear, O Israel, the Lord our God, the
Lord is one.

"Praised be His name, whose glorious kingdom is for ever and ever.

"You shall love the Lord your God, with
all your heart, and with all your soul.

"And these words which I command you
this day, shall be upon your heart. You shall

teach them to your children, and you shall speak of them when you sit in your house, and when you are on the road; when you lie down, and when you awake. And you shall bind them as a sign upon your hand, and they shall be for frontlets between your eyes. And you shall write them upon the door-posts of your house and upon your gates.

"Praised be the Lord by day; praised be the Lord by night. Praised be the Lord when we lie down to sleep; praised be the Lord when we awake.

"I am in the care of the Lord, when I sleep and when I awake.

"In Thy help I trust, O Lord."

WASHING THE HANDS BEFORE MEALS Our great sages have decreed that men and women and children must wash their hands well and remove all uncleanliness from them before partaking of food. The wisdom and value of the practice of washing the hands before meals is too obvious to need comment. But Judaism, to make the practice more impressive, elevates it to the dignity of a religious ceremony, and for this reason has instituted a special benediction to be said immediately before drying the hands after such washing:

בָּרוּךְ אַתָּה יְהֹוָה אֱלֹהֵינוּ, מֶלֶךְ הָעוֹלָם, אֲשֶׁר קִדְּשָׁנוּ בְּמִצְוֹתָיו,
וְצִוָּנוּ עַל נְטִילַת יָדָיִם.

"Barukh attah adonai, elohenu, melekh haolam, asher kidshanu bemitzvotav, vetzivanu al netilat yadayim.

"Praised be Thou, O Lord our God, King of the universe, who hast sanctified us by Thy commandments, and hast commanded us concerning the washing of hands."

GRACE AT MEALS Our tables may be turned into altars of God, if the food we put upon them is *kosher,* and if God's name is mentioned at meals. According to the Jewish religion, eating is more than just a necessary process for keeping alive. It partakes of the nature of sacrifice and is invested with the nature of holiness. Our sages therefore ordained that immediately after drying the hands before meals, one should take a morsel of bread, and before eating it say:

בָּרוּךְ אַתָּה יְהֹוָה אֱלֹהֵינוּ, מֶלֶךְ הָעוֹלָם, הַמּוֹצִיא לֶחֶם מִן הָאָרֶץ.

"Barukh attah adonai, elohenu, melekh haolam, hamotzi lehem min haaretz."

"Praised be Thou, O Lord our God, King

of the universe, who bringest forth bread from
the earth."

After the meal is over, we thank the Lord
our God for having provided us and the other
creatures of the world with food. The *grace*
which men, women and children recite after
meals, is to be found in any Prayer Book.
That such gratitude must be expressed, was
commanded by the Lord our God: "When
thou hast eaten and been satisfied, thou shalt
bless the Lord thy God."

BENEDICTIONS Our sages teach us that no man
has the right to deny himself the
legitimate pleasures of life. Everyone, according to the will of our Creator, must enjoy
the bounties of the creation. In appreciation
of God's creation of such enjoyments, the Jews
have for many centuries uttered a benediction
before enjoying them.

There are benedictions to be said on many
occasions, which can be found in any of the
Prayer Books. The following are the benedictions of gratitude for the produce of the soil,
which are used in our everyday life:

Before eating fruit which grows on trees:

בָּרוּךְ אַתָּה יְהֹוָה אֱלֹהֵינוּ, מֶלֶךְ הָעוֹלָם, בּוֹרֵא פְּרִי הָעֵץ.

[85]

"Barukh attah adonai, elohenu melekh haolam, bore peri haetz."

"Praised be Thou, O Lord our God, King of the universe, who createst the fruit of the tree."

Before eating fruit which grows on the ground:

בָּרוּךְ אַתָּה יְהֹוָה אֱלֹהֵינוּ, מֶלֶךְ הָעוֹלָם, בּוֹרֵא פְּרִי הָאֲדָמָה.

"Barukh attah adonai, elohenu melekh haolam, bore peri haadamah."

"Praised be Thou, O Lord our God, King of the universe, who createst the fruit of the earth."

Before eating food, other than bread, prepared from either wheat, barley, rye, oats, or spelt:

בָּרוּךְ אַתָּה יְהֹוָה אֱלֹהֵינוּ, מֶלֶךְ הָעוֹלָם, בּוֹרֵא מִינֵי מְזוֹנוֹת.

"Barukh attah adonai, elohenu melekh haolam, bore mine mezonot."

"Praised be Thou, O Lord our God, King of the universe, who createst various kinds of food."

Before drinking wine:

בָּרוּךְ אַתָּה יְהֹוָה אֱלֹהֵינוּ, מֶלֶךְ הָעוֹלָם, בּוֹרֵא פְּרִי הַגָּפָן.

"Barukh attah adonai, elohenu melekh haolam, bore peri hagaphen."

"Praised be Thou, O Lord our God, King of the universe, who createst the fruit of the vine."

Before eating meat, fish, eggs, or dairy products, or drinking any beverage except wine:

בָּרוּךְ אַתָּה יְהֹוָה אֱלֹהֵינוּ, מֶלֶךְ הָעוֹלָם, שֶׁהַכֹּל נִהְיֶה בִּדְבָרוֹ.

"Barukh attah adonai, elohenu melekh haolam shehakol niheyeh bidvaro."

"Praised be Thou, O Lord our God, King of the universe, by whose word all things exist."

KOSHER FOOD According to the Holy Scriptures, when the first human being was created by the hand of the Almighty, he was given permission by the Creator to consume for his own needs "every herb yielding seed, and the fruit of trees yielding seed." Later on, when Noah left the Ark after the flood, the Almighty gave man permission to use all living things for food, on the condition, however, that he did not eat flesh with its life, which is the blood.

Later still, in the Mosaic Law, the Almighty forbade the use of certain classes of animals as food. The reason given by the

Almighty for this decree is couched in the following words: "Ye shall therefore separate between the clean beast and the unclean, and between the unclean fowl and the clean; and ye shall not make your souls detestable by beast, or by fowl, or by anything wherewith the ground teemeth, which I have set apart for you to hold unclean. And ye shall be holy unto Me; for I the Lord am holy, and have set you apart from the peoples, that ye should be Mine."

The reason, then, why we must abstain from eating the flesh of these particular animals is simply given by the Almighty, that since He Himself is holy, and since He set us aside from all peoples to be His, we too must be holy and not eat the flesh of animals which He declared to be unclean. But why these animals are unclean is not stated.

Again, when bidding us not to eat *terephah,* meat of animals that were torn by beasts, the Almighty stated: "And ye shall be holy men unto Me; therefore ye shall not eat flesh that is torn of beasts in the field; ye shall cast it to the dogs." It is evident, then, that it was His will that the Jews, as His selected people, must for the sake of holiness abstain from eating meat indiscriminately.

Man, to approach the holiness of God, had

to be weaned away from brutally killing things
that have life in order to satisfy his thirst for
blood. Taking the life of harmless animals to
satisfy man's appetite and lust is abhorrent in
the sight of the Almighty whose mercy is over
all His creatures. But instinctively and inher-
ently man was and still is a flesh-eater, and he
therefore could not be easily torn from his natural habits by the utterance of a single command. For this reason the Almighty placed restrictions on the use of flesh as food. And
gradually the restrictions became so numerous
in the Jewish religion that the eating of meat
became a regular ritual.

Meals among the Jews are not measured
merely by physical desires and esthetic sense,
but also by its spiritual values. The Jew must
sanctify his life by means of his every day needs,
in order to be holy in the sight of his God.

It is therefore absolutely necessary for Jewish women to become thoroughly familiar with
the law relating to *kosher* and forbidden foods.
It is their responsibility to provide their families
with food that is not forbidden by Jewish law.

In the Five Books of Moses, which contain
the written Law of God, there is a long list
of animals which are considered unclean and

unfit for use by the Jewish people, who accepted the Torah from God.

In addition to the Law of God as expressly recorded in the Torah, there was a traditional law dealing with the dietary regulations, which was handed down from the time of Moses, by word of mouth, to the time of the Talmud, when it was formulated by the scholars and written down. A Jewish home cannot be considered as *kosher*, unless the mistress of the house observes all the laws that are recorded in the Five Books of Moses as well as those that were written down in the Talmud. The most important of these traditional laws are given in this Chapter.

Meat is *kosher*, ritually fit for use: When it comes from the animals designated in the Torah as being *clean*; when the animal was ritually slaughtered by a *shohet*, a man permitted by license to perform the killing of animals and fowl in accordance with the prescribed laws; when after the ritual slaughter, the animal was opened and examined by the *shohet*, and found to have no fatal disease; when the meat was properly purged, that is, all the forbidden fat and blood-vessels have been removed; and, finally, when the meat was properly soaked in water and salted as required by law.

Poultry, too, must be opened after slaughtering, and examined. (See "How to Prepare Fowl," page 98).

Buy your meat from a butcher who is religious and dependable. A lax or unscrupulous butcher may render *kosher* meat unfit for use by mere neglect of duty. For instance, he may fail to remove all the forbidden fat and blood-vessels from the meat; or he may neglect to purge it, or to sprinkle water on it three full days after the animal has been slaughtered.

The blood of all animals is forbidden except that of fish. Nevertheless, it is inadvisable to collect the blood of fish into a single vessel for the purpose of using it, as people may suspect you of using blood which is forbidden by law. In Jewish law, certain things are at times forbidden not on strict principles of law, but merely for the sake of avoiding the possibility of arousing suspicion.

LAWS CONCERNING FORBIDDEN FOOD By the law of God, any meat of animals that have cloven hoofs but do not chew the cud, or of those who chew the cud but have no cloven hoofs, is *terephah*, unfit for use by Jewish people. Concerning ham, bacon, and other hog meat, there is a specific commandment in the Law of Moses: "And the swine, though it has cloven hoofs, but since it cheweth not the cud, it shall be unclean to you."

The hindquarter part of even a clean animal may not be used, unless the forbidden parts and the blood-vessels are properly removed. Most butchers know how to purge only the forequarters of *kosher* animals, but not the hindquarters. The Jews therefore use the forequarter meat only, and abstain from using the hindquarter meat.

All kinds of shell-fish, such as oysters, clams, lobsters, crabs and others, as well as all creeping things, are forbidden by the Law of God, as recorded in the Five Books of Moses.

Fish that have no fins and removable scales are forbidden by the Law of Moses. All fishes have fins, but not all fishes have scales that can be removed. Any product made of unclean fish is equally forbidden. Therefore, when buying oil and fish roe, great care should be exercised to obtain only that which comes of clean fish. Caviare prepared of the roe of sturgeon is forbidden.

The Law of Moses lists twenty-four kinds of fowl, the meat of which is forbidden to Jews (Leviticus xi, 13-19). The most com-

mon among them are: The vulture, eagle,
raven, ostrich, owl and bat. Eggs of forbidden birds may not be used. Jewish housewives
should, therefore, abstain from buying liquid
eggs unless they know their origin. The general shape of *kosher* eggs is broadly rounded
at one end and tapering at the other.

The prohibition against eating blood has
been extended even to eggs, and the blood found
in them is forbidden. Some blood-specks may
be removed from the eggs, thus rendering the
egg suitable for use, and in other cases they
may not be removed and the whole egg must
be discarded. It is therefore best to open all
eggs separately and examine them thoroughly
to ascertain if they contain blood-specks before
using them in the preparation of food. If the
eggs contain blood-specks and you do not wish
to discard them, you must consult a competent
Rabbi about what to do with them.

The Jewish law strictly forbids one to eat
food containing worms or mites, or food that is
worm-eaten. Before boiling dried peas or beans,
or any other food that generally contains parts
that are worm-eaten, you must carefully pick
out and discard all those that are worm-eaten.

Many kinds of vegetables, such as lettuce,
scallions, green peas, string beans, and cucum-

bers contain worms and are usually covered with insects. These may neither be eaten raw nor put in the pot to be boiled without first being thoroughly examined and washed.

The use of berries shall be limited, because most of them are infected with worms and bugs. If one desires to use them, one must first examine each berry thoroughly.

Worms are often found in the interior of fish, especially in the brain, liver, intestines, mouth and ears. Haddock is most susceptible to worms. The places where worms are likely to be found must be thoroughly examined before using the fish.

All fruits generally contain worms, and therefore require examination before being eaten or cooked. Before cooking, the fruit must be opened one by one and the stones removed, in order that the examination may be thorough. The worm-eaten parts must be cut out and discarded.

If, in cutting fruit or vegetables, you happen to cut up a worm, you must wipe the knife well, and cut out and discard that part of the fruit or vegetable where the worm had been cut.

The black spot, sometimes found in fruits and in such vegetables as peas, is the breeding place of the worm and may not be eaten. When such spots are found in fruits, they may be cut out and the rest of the fruit may be eaten; but when found in peas, beans and lentils, the whole vegetable must be discarded.

Flour and cereals containing large worms or insects may be rendered fit for use by being sifted through a sieve. But flour and cereals containing mites, must be entirely discarded, as the mites will also pass through the sieve.

To determine whether a given food contains mites, spread some of the food on a slightly warmed plate. If mites are present, they will creep to the surface.

Water from wells or rivers known to be infested with worms or insects may be used for drinking or cooking only after it has been well filtered. Filtering is also necessary before such water may be used for the purpose of soaking meat or washing any article of food. The filter must be a finely spun cloth capable of excluding even the smallest insect.

If in doubt about the violation of any of these rules of law, consult a competent Rabbi. Do not presume to decide these questions yourself.

LAWS CONCERNING THE SOAKING OF MEAT Our Father in heaven was very emphatic in His command to the Jews not to eat the blood of animals or fowl. He repeated this command several times in His Law. The blood is called the *life* or *soul* of the animate being. Our Talmudic sages have accordingly laid down the law that in order to remove effectively the blood from the meat, the meat must first be soaked in water to open the pores, and then salted to draw the blood out.

The meat must be soaked and entirely submerged in water for a full half hour. Wherever a particle of blood is visible on the meat, it must be thoroughly washed off with the water in which the meat is soaking. In the case of fowl, the place where the incision was made in killing it, must be thoroughly washed, and the blood visible inside the fowl must be washed off.

The meat should not be soaked in very cold water, lest it becomes so hardened that the blood will not easily emerge when the meat is salted. Neither should the water be too warm, because it would tend to harden the blood in the meat.

Before the approach of the Sabbath, if one

is pressed for time, the meat need not be soaked for a full half hour. It suffices to wash the meat thoroughly and then let it soak in the water for a short time; when the water no longer becomes reddened by the blood, the meat may be salted.

Frozen meat must be allowed to thaw out, before being soaked, but it should not be placed near a hot stove nor put in hot water, lest the blood become hardened. In cases of emergency, the frozen meat may be put in tepid water.

The head of cattle must be removed before soaking it in water. The head must be split open, the brain removed, and the membrane upon it rent before it is soaked. The head must be soaked separately, not together with other meat.

The tips of the hoofs of animals must be cut before soaking the legs in water, so that the blood can flow out. If the tips of the hoofs were not cut before soaking the legs, a competent Rabbi should be consulted for an opinion.

The heart of an animal must be cut open before soaking it in water, so that the blood may issue from it.

Some people, before soaking the lungs of an animal, cut them and lay open the large tubes.

Before soaking the spleen, the surrounding membrane and the spleenic veins must be removed. The spleenic vein should be pulled out by its head along with the three cords that are contained in it. If any of the three cords happen to become severed, it is necessary to remove it from its root.

Unsalted and unsoaked meat must not be put in a place where salt is sometimes kept. A special vessel in which to keep un-*kashered* (unsoaked and unsalted) meat must be set aside. Food which is generally eaten without first being washed must not be put in this vessel lest it become contaminated with the blood of the un-*kashered* meat.

The vessel used for the purpose of soaking meat may not be used for the preparation of any other food.

If one should by error allow meat to remain soaking in the water for twenty-four hours, the meat as well as the vessel in which it has been soaked become unfit for use. In that event it is best to consult a competent Rabbi.

HOW TO PREPARE A FOWL

In preparing a fowl for soaking, the following rules must be observed:

1. When singeing the feathers of poultry, care should be taken that it be done over a small flame. The poultry should

be constantly moved to and fro over the flame, so that the heat may not harden the blood.

2. The head must be severed.

3. The loose skin around the neck must be removed or turned, and the congealed blood wiped and washed away.

4. The gullet and windpipe should be thrown away, and since the jugular vein has been cut in two, care should be taken to pull out both parts.

5. Two bloodveins in the neck which can easily be seen should be removed, and the third one which lies embedded in the flesh and runs along the front groove of the neck, should either be lifted by the edge of a knife and drawn out, or cut across several times.

6. The tips of the claws and the wings should be cut away, so as to expose the inner flesh.

7. The fowl must be properly opened, and the inner parts must be carefully examined for any irregularity.

8. You must ascertain definitely that the intestines are clear of tumors and swellings.

9. The gall must be carefully looked for.

10. The lungs should be forced away from the ribs and discarded.

11. It is also best to discard the heart.

If it is to be used, the tips at both ends must be cut off, and the heart cut across several times.

12. The gizzard should be cut open, and the inner wrinkled lining peeled away and examined to ascertain that there is no nail, needle, pin, or wire embedded in the flesh. Should any such irregularity be found, a competent Rabbi should be consulted.

13. Should any irregularity be found in the fowl, such as a broken wing, rib or thigh; diseased entrails or liver; any growth or swelling; wire, pin or nail embedded in the flesh; or the gall missing, a qualified Rabbi should be consulted to ascertain whether or not the fowl is *kosher,* fit for use.

LAWS CONCERNING THE SALTING OF MEAT After the meat has been kept in water for the required length of time, it is taken out and put on a special board for salting. Before salting the meat, some of the water should be allowed to drain off, because if the meat is too wet, the salt will dissolve at once, and if too dry the salt will not adhere to it at all. In either case the salt would fail to drain the blood from the meat.

The salt should be coarser than flour so

that it may not dissolve too quickly, but not so coarse that it will entirely drop from the meat. The salt must be kept dry so that it can be easily sprinkled.

The salting board must be placed in an oblique position, so that the blood may flow down freely. This board should either be made of wicker, or be perforated or grooved, to allow free draining. A hollow receptacle should by no means be used, nor a board with a hollow part or cavity where the brine may accumulate.

The salt must be sprinkled on all sides of the meat, and in all cuts and folds, so that no part of the surface is left unsalted. Care should be taken to open poultry properly so that it may be well salted within.

If a piece of meat is cut up again after soaking, the new surfaces produced by the cut must be washed clean of surface-blood before being salted.

Poultry or meat having a cavity must be turned with the hollow part downward when placed on the board after salting, in order that the blood may drain freely.

Meat-bones must be soaked and salted like meat.

Bones which contain marrow and have meat clinging to them may be salted together with other meat; but if the bones are bare, they should not be salted together with other meat, and should not even be placed near other meat while in the salt.

The head and the brains must be salted separately from other meat. The head may be salted while it still has the hair on it.

It is permissible to salt the legs of an animal without removing the hair. While in the salt, the legs must be placed hoof-downward, so that the blood can drain out easily.

The meat should remain in the salt for one hour; but in cases of emergency twenty-four minutes will suffice.

Should the meat accidentally be allowed to remain in the salt a whole day, or if, while in the salt, it should fall to the ground, a competent Rabbi should be consulted.

After the meat has remained in salt for the proper length of time, the salt should be thoroughly shaken off and the meat washed three times in the following manner: Spill water on it, then wash it in a vessel containing water, then spill water on it again. Never put the meat immediately after salting into a dry vessel before it is ritually purged. Water must be poured into the vessel—after the spilling of water on the meat—before the meat may be washed in it.

Eggs found in poultry, no matter what their stage of development, must be soaked, salted, and purged as if it were meat. They must not, however, be salted together with meat, and they must not be placed in a position where meat blood can drain on them. Such eggs must not be eaten or boiled together with milk or any other dairy products, because they are considered as meat.

Liver, because it contains a large quantity of blood, may not be made *kosher* (fit for use) in the same manner as ordinary meat. It must first be rent asunder, or well pierced several times with a knife, and then broiled over a fire. Before the liver is placed on the flame, it must be purged, and while being broiled it must be lightly sprinkled with salt. After broiling, it should be purged three times of the blood which has been discharged. It may then be either eaten as is or broiled.

Liver must be broiled either over a flame or over hot coals. When being broiled it must not be wrapped in paper, and the open parts must be kept in a downward position so that the blood may drain from them.

Steaks, chops or any other kind of meat

intended for broiling, must first be purged and sprinkled with a little salt. After broiling, the blood must be washed off by purging the meat three times, as in the case of liver. It may then be heated again on the fire if desired.

Meat that remains unsoaked and unsalted for three full days after the animal has been ritually slaughtered, may not be used for boiling purposes, as it no longer can be made fit for use by soaking and salting. It may be broiled and thereafter eaten as is, but it may not be boiled. If, however, the meat has been either soaked in water or purged before the three days were over, it may be soaked and salted and then boiled.

MEAT AND MILK One is strictly forbidden by Jewish law to eat or boil meat and dairy products together. In certain instances, it is not even permissible to derive any benefit from meat that has been mixed with dairy products. Whenever, therefore, meat and dairy products happen to become mixed, a Rabbi should be consulted.

Two sets of dishes, kitchen utensils, table cloths, and dish towels must be kept in every Jewish home, one set for meat and the other for dairy products. The two sets must be of different and distinct patterns or designs, so that they may not be interchanged one for the other. In cases where the patterns are similar, distinguishing marks must be made.

It is not proper to cook both dairy products and meat in a closed oven, on a range or open gas-stove, without covering the pots in which they are cooked. Care should be taken to separate the pots sufficiently so that one may not boil over or splash into the other.

If you happen to boil meat in a milk pot, or vice versa; or cover hot meat with a lid used for milk, or vice versa; or stir meat food with a milk spoon, or vice versa, consult a competent Rabbi about what should be done.

As bread is eaten with both milk and meat, it should not contain either milk or meat products, unless it is intended for such meals only and its special character is clearly indicated.

Never wash meat and milk dishes together, and never use soap or powder for washing dishes, unless you know that it is *kosher* for that purpose.

If one should cut an onion or some other pungent thing with a knife used for meat, and put it in food made of milk products, or vice versa, a competent Rabbi should be consulted.

After eating meat, which takes a long time to digest, one should wait six hours before eating dairy food.

It is permissible to partake of dairy food immediately after eating food which has been prepared with neither meat nor meat-fat, but which has been boiled in a pot used for boiling meat, even if the pot had not been thoroughly cleansed beforehand.

Meat may be eaten immediately after dairy products, for the latter are generally light and esaily digestible. After eating cheese, which clings to the teeth, one must rinse one's mouth well, and wash one's hands before eating meat. If one eats hardened cheese, one must wait six hours before eating meat.

If one desires to eat meat after eating cheese, one must remove the table-cloth upon which the cheese was served, and must also remove from the table the rest of the bread that was eaten with the cheese.

IMMERSION OF VESSELS Ordinary dishes and utensils to be used in the Jewish home must be sanctified for the purpose. It is customary to immerse all new vessels and dishes made of glass or metal or containing metal parts, in running water, and to pronounce the follow-ing benediction before the immersion.

בָּרוּךְ אַתָּה יְהֹוָה אֱלֹהֵינוּ, מֶלֶךְ הָעוֹלָם, אֲשֶׁר קִדְּשָׁנוּ בְּמִצְוֹתָיו,
וְצִוָּנוּ עַל טְבִילַת כֵּלִים.

"Barukh attah adonai, elohenu melekh haolam, asher kidshanu bemitzvotav, vetzivanu al tebilat kelim."

"Praised be Thou, O Lord our God King of the universe, who hast sanctified us by Thy commandments, and hast commanded us con-cerning the immersion of vessels."

THE FIRST OF THE DOUGH (HALLAH) Most of the Jewish symbols and ceremonies are connected with the cherished memories of the Jewish past, when the Jew enjoyed inde-pendence as a nation in his home-land and practiced the impressive rites in the Temple at Jerusalem.

In the Holy Scriptures, the following divine command is written: "From the first of your dough shall you give unto the Lord as a heave-offering." When the Temple was in existence, this heave-offering, known as *hallah,* was given to the priest. The Jewish concept was that all our possessions belong to the Almighty and there-fore must be consecrated to His service. Since we must make use of our possessions, the Almighty decreed that by dedicating a part of them the remainder is released for our own use.

Ever since the destruction of the Temple, the fulfillment of the precept to set aside the first of the dough, *hallah,* was included in the three duties entirely devolving upon the Jewish woman. As the mistress of the house, the Jewish woman separates a portion of the dough from that which she is preparing for baking.

Tradition says that the woman was entrusted with the performance of this holy act of separating the first of the dough, because of her origin at the creation of the world. Mother-earth, according to this tradition, at the very beginning, gave up a portion of her body out of which the Almighty formed spiritual man. Thereafter, man yielded part of his body, a rib, out of which the Creator fashioned woman, as if she were a *hallah*-portion of man. She was then given back to man as the *gift* of the Lord, to be a noble and sublime companion to him. Through the ages, therefore, the Jewish woman re-enacts her origin at the creation and sets apart the dough which is a *gift* unto the Lord. She is to exert a holy influence in the home which she directs. She is to hallow the bread, she is to hallow the life in the home. She is to make her kitchen a Temple of God, and of her table an altar.

Immediately before separating the *hallah,* the following benediction is recited:

בָּרוּךְ אַתָּה יְהֹוָה אֱלֹהֵינוּ, מֶלֶךְ הָעוֹלָם, אֲשֶׁר קִדְּשָׁנוּ בְּמִצְוֹתָיו, וְצִוָּנוּ לְהַפְרִישׁ חַלָּה.

"Barukh attah adonai, elohenu melekh haolam, asher kidshanu bemitzvotav, vetzivanu lehaphrish hallah."

"Praised be Thou, O Lord our God, King of the universe, who hast sanctified us by Thy commandments, and hast commanded us to separate *hallah.*"

After the separation of the dough, the following is recited.

"May it be Thy will, O Lord our God and God of our fathers, that the Temple be speedily rebuilt in our days. And there we will serve Thee with awe and reverence as in the days of old and as in ancient years."

The law of separating the *hallah*-portion applies only to dough made out of the five species: Wheat, barley, spelt, rye, and oats.

The quantity of the flour kneaded into dough which becomes subject to the law of *hallah* is no less than the equivalent of the weight of forty-three and one-fifth eggs, or two and a half quarts, or three and one-half pounds. There is no mention in the Law of Moses as to how much of the dough should be separated as *hallah*, but the limit is prescribed by the Rabbis to be no less than the size of an olive.

The separated portion of the dough must be burnt. The custom is to burn it in the oven with the baking bread.

Only dough kneaded for the purpose of baking requires the separation of *hallah* with the recitation of the benediction. If dough is prepared for cooking, or frying, or for any other purpose besides baking, the *hallah* should be separated without saying the benediction. If, however, any part of such dough is intended to be used for baking, the benediction must be said.

Only dough kneaded with water requires the separation of *hallah*. If one intends to knead the dough with eggs or with any kind of fruit-juice or milk, it is best to add a little water to it while kneading the dough, so that the *hallah* may be separated from it and the proper benediction pronounced.

The ready-made *matzah*, unleavened bread, bought for the Passover, should be placed either in one vessel, or tied up in one cloth or sheet, and a part of it separated as *hallah* while pronouncing the necessary benediction.

If the separation of the *hallah* from the dough has been omitted through negligence, then the baked product should either be placed in one receptacle or wrapped in or covered with a cloth and a piece of one of the baked products should be broken off while pronouncing the necessary benediction. The piece thus broken off shall then be burnt.

The rite of performing the separation of the dough cannot take place on the Sabbath. Therefore if it should become known on the Sabbath that no *hallah* has been separated from the bread to be eaten that day, a piece of each loaf then used must be left over. At the conclusion of the Sabbath, these pieces should be placed in one receptacle, and out of them a small piece, no less than the size of an olive, should be separated as *hallah*, while pronouncing the necessary benediction. The separated piece should then be burnt.

SABBATH

THE JEWISH DAY OF REST

"Happy is the man that doeth this, and the son of man that holdeth fast by it: that keepeth the Sabbath from profaning it, and keepeth his hand from doing any evil."

(ISAIAH LVI, 2).

SABBATH

THE JEWISH DAY OF REST

IMPORTANCE OF SABBATH *"Remember the Sabbath day to keep it holy. Six days shalt thou labor, and do all thy work; but the seventh day is a Sabbath to the Lord thy God, in it thou shalt not do any manner of work, thou, nor thy son, nor thy daughter, nor thy man-servant, nor thy maid-servant, nor thy cattle, nor the stranger that is within thy gates; for in six days the Lord made heaven and earth, the sea, and all that in them is, and rested on the seventh day; therefore the Lord blessed the Sabbath-day, and hallowed it."*

This is the fourth of the Ten Commandments.

Our Rabbis say that when God was about to give this commandment to the Jews, he said to Moses: "I have a precious gift stored away in My treasures, and its name is *Sabbath*. I desire to give this gift to the Israelites. Go and apprise them of it."

The Sabbath is, indeed, the most beautiful

gift Israel received from God—the day of rest, which was in later years adopted by the rest of the world. It was considered so important in the sight of the Almighty, that several times in His Law He admonished the Jews to observe it.

As far back as the days of the early prophets, the observance of the Sabbath was already considered of prime importance in the life of the Jewish people. All the prophets from Isaiah and Jeremiah to Nehemiah eloquently urged the Jewish people to observe carefully their day of rest, the Sabbath.

Later on in Jewish history, the leaders of Jewish thought, the Talmudic authorities, considered the observance of the Sabbath as the foundation of the Jewish faith. Two major volumes in the Talmud are devoted exclusively to the laws and regulations concerning the observance of the Sabbath; and numerous legends, proverbs, laws and stories about this day of rest are scattered throughout the other treatises of the Talmud and the Midrash.

The following are quotations from the Talmud concerning the Sabbath:

"Great is the Sabbath, for it outweighs all the other commandments of God."

"Whosoever keeps the Sabbath-day holy is protected against temptation to sin."

"Jerusalem was destroyed by the enemy for no other reason than the one that the Jews desecrated the Sabbath."

"If the Jews were to observe two Sabbaths properly, they would at once be redeemed; even if one Sabbath were rightly kept, the Messiah would appear."

"On the Sabbath, man is endowed with an additional soul, which is taken away from him at the conclusion of the Sabbath."

SABBATH THE BRIDE A poetic and beautiful idea about the Sabbath was conceived by our Talmudic sages. They said that the Jews were wedded to the Sabbath, the Jews being the bridegroom and Sabbath the bride. They described how the wedding between the Jews and the Sabbath took place:

"When the seventh day of the creation was consecrated by God as the Sabbath, the Holy Day of rest, it complained: 'O mighty Lord, every day of the week is associated with one another: Sunday is associated with Monday; Tuesday with Wednesday; and Thursday with Friday; but I stand alone, without an associate.' God replied: 'I have provided an associate for you: a true bridegroom.' 'Who may that be?' asked Sabbath. 'None other,' replied God, 'than

My people Israel. You shall be the bride, and My people the bridegroom.' "

Every Jew must therefore rejoice with the coming of the Sabbath. The mere expectation of a distinguished guest would make him active in setting his house in order; how much more so when that guest is Queen Sabbath! The pious Jewish woman, in expectation of receiving the Sabbath, busies herself with many things on Friday. She polishes the silverware and other utensils to be used for and on the Sabbath; she puts fresh coverings on the beds, arranges the household furniture, and covers the table with a fresh, white cloth, which remains on the table to the end of the Sabbath.

In honor of the Sabbath, everybody must wash one's face and hands and bathe one's feet in warm water; and if one possesses the facilities, one should bathe the whole body in warm water. Our sages say that everybody should try to wear fine clothes especially set aside for the Sabbath, and, if possible, not to wear the same clothes as on weekdays.

Note how our great sages of old received the Sabbath-bride: Rabbi Haninah used to wrap himself in his festive cloak and stand ready, on Friday toward evening, saying: "Come ye, and let us go forth to meet Queen Sabbath."

Rabbi Yannai would put on his best Sabbath clothes and would say: "Come, O bride; Come, O bride."

In the sixteenth century a beautiful poem was composed by Rabbi Solomn Alkabiz, entitled 'Lekah Dodi,' *Come my Beloved,* which was incorporated in our Friday evening services. This poem, opening with an invitation to friends to welcome the bride Sabbath, is full of courage and hope for the oppressed Jewish people.

PREPARING FOR THE SABBATH "And thou shalt call the Sabbath *oneg* (pleasure)," are the words of the Almighty through His prophet Isaiah. And our sages ask: "How is the Sabbath to be observed as a day of pleasure?" And they reply: "With good food and drink, with clean and becoming clothes, with joy and entertainment; and for this you will receive reward from Heaven."

It is therefore the duty of everybody to rise early on Friday to make the purchases necessary for a worthy celebration of the Sabbath. The more one spends the greater the merit. No one should stint in making preparations for the Sabbath, but should procure choice meat, fish, dessert and good wine, in accordance with one's means.

Even a poor man should economize the whole week in order to save up enough money to buy food in honor of the Sabbath. If necessary, one should borrow money, and even pledge one's personal property as security, in order to provide for the Sabbath. Our Rabbis say: "The Holy One, praised be He, said to the Israelites: 'My children, borrow for My sake and sanctify the holy day; and have confidence in Me that I will repay it.' "

Our Talmudic sages also maintain that expenses incurred for a joyful Sabbath celebration do not impoverish, but on the contrary enrich those who spend beyond their means to enjoy the Sabbath. To prove this, the sages handed down a beautiful story of a certain man who was known to the people of his town as "Joseph, the honorer of Sabbath." He was called that because he used to live in extreme poverty all week, saving all his meager earnings until the Sabbath when he would spend it all for good food in honor of that day.

Joseph had an extremely rich non-Jewish neighbor, who was as superstitious as he was rich. One day Joseph's neighbor consulted a fortune-teller, and was told that all his wealth would one day become the property of Joseph. He was so frightened by the fortune-teller's words that he couldn't sleep, but sat up nights thinking of how to avoid the calamity foretold to him. He finally hit upon a scheme which he thought would be perfect and safe.

He sold all his possessions, and with that money he bought the most costly gem that could be found in the whole world. This precious gem he carefully sewed up in the lining of his turban.

"Now," said he with a self-satisfied smile, "my Jewish neighbor can never possess my wealth."

Once, as the proud possessor of the precious gem was crossing a bridge, a strong gust of wind carried off his turban into the stream where it sank to the bottom. After many hours of futile search for the turban, the loser of the gem consoled himself: "My loss is great; I am now poor and penniless, but at least I am certain that my wealth will not fall into the hands of the Jew."

Time passed, and the precious gem became loosened from the lining of the turban and was swallowed by a fish. Late one Friday afternoon, some fishermen, on drawing up their net from the stream, found it empty but for one beautiful fish which they brought to town for sale. "Who will buy this beautiful fish from us?" inquired the fishermen from the passers-by. "Because it is late in the afternoon, we are ready to sell it at a sacrifice."

No one paid attention to the fishermen's offer, because everybody had already been fully prepared for the Sabbath. At last one of the passers-by suggested to the fishermen: "Go to the house of Joseph, the Honorer of Sabbath; he never refuses to buy anything offered to him on Friday with which he can honor the Sabbath."

Accordingly, the fishermen went and offered the fish to Joseph who bought it from them at their price. On cutting the fish open, the pious man was greatly surprised by the presence of the precious gem. The Sabbath over, he sold the gem for a huge sum of money.

Joseph was afterwards met by an old man (said to be the prophet Elijah) who said: "Him who lends to the Sabbath, by incurring additional expenses in honoring the Sabbath, the Sabbath will repay."

Although it is a meritorious act to enjoy good food on the Sabbath, yet it is even more important to provide the poor with all that they may require for the Sabbath. If one can afford to provide the needy, but fails to do so, and merely makes an elaborate meal for one's family in honor of the Sabbath, one's consuming of good food is no longer considered a *mitzvah*, a fulfillment of God's will, but mere gluttony.

The Talmudic sages say that Ezra, upon returning to Palestine from the Babylonian captivity (459 B. C. E.), instituted many important ordinances for the good of the Jewish people. One of these ordinances bids the woman to rise early on Friday morning and bake bread to supply the poor with *hallot*, white loaves of bread, for the Sabbath.

No matter how many servants one may have, it is the duty of every man and woman personally to honor the Sabbath. Even our great scholars, in Talmudic times, themselves did some work in honor of the Sabbath. Rabbi Hisda, for instance, so the Talmud records, used to cut the vegetables very fine for the Sabbath. Rabbah and Rab Joseph used to chop wood for cooking. Rab Zera was in the habit of lighting the fire over which the Sabbath food was cooked. Rab Nahman used to put the house in order, bringing in all the utensils needed for the Sabbath and putting away the things used only during week-days.

THE
LIGHTING
OF THE
CANDLES

While it is still daylight, the table should be set for the evening meal with the best cutlery and tablewear in the house. In the middle of the table should be placed the Sabbath *menorah,* or candlesticks, provided with candles. Near the candlesticks is generally placed a bottle of sparkling red wine, with a silver or gold goblet over which the *kiddush* (Sanctification Prayer) is to be chanted. Two *hallot* (white loaves of bread) covered with a napkin often specially embroidered for the purpose, should be placed before the seat of the master of the house.

Everybody, men as well as women, are obliged to light the Sabbath candles in honor of the Sabbath. However, the fulfillment of this duty was left to the Jewish woman, and by her lighting the candles she exempts all other members of the household from performing this precept.

Light, symbolic of the precepts and the Torah, beautifies and adorns the Sabbath and makes it appear more restful and holy. Therefore some women light one candle for each member of the family; some use a seven-branched *menorah*: but the more candles lit the more meritorious. In no event should less than two candles be lit for the occasion.

Should you but once neglect to light the Sabbath candles, you should, all your lifetime, add one extra candle every Friday to the number you previously used to light. This rule of law does not apply to a case where you were prevented from lighting the candles by an accident.

Praiseworthy are those women who wash themselves, dress their hair, pare and polish their nails, and put on their best Sabbath apparel before lighting the Sabbath candles. If, however, a woman is delayed by her occupation and reaches home about half an hour before sundown, it is best for her to attend to the lighting of the candles at once without changing her apparel, because one must always avoid the possibility of profaning the Sabbath.

The candles should be lit before sunset. To avoid error it is best to light the candles about one half hour before sundown.

Some Jewish women, in their eagerness to observe the *mitzvah* (precept) of lighting the Sabbath candles, light them even after sunset in the event of delay. This grave error is, of course, due to ignorance. It is a serious sin to light candles after sunset. And it is particularly loathsome in the sight of the Almighty when so grave a transgression is committed for the purpose of fulfilling His command.

Some pious Jewish women observe the beautiful custom of giving charity before lighting the candles.

It is necessary that the two *hallot* (white loaves of bread) be placed upon the table and covered with a napkin before lighting the candles.

The candles should be lit in the room and on the table where meals are generally served, in order that it may be apparent that the candles were lit in honor of the Sabbath.

After lighting the candles, the woman puts her hands before her face before saying the benediction. The benediction over, she removes her hands and gazes at the light. False reasons have been advanced by some authors for this procedure, which is in reality not a mere matter of custom, but required by law.

The Jewish law states that a benediction must be said immediately before a precept is performed. According to this law, then, the benediction for the lighting of the Sabbath candles should be said before lighting them. This, however, is impossible since by pronouncing the benediction one assumes the holiness and the observance of the Sabbath, after which one is no longer allowed to light the candles. To comply with the law requiring a benediction before the performance of a precept—in this case the lighting of the candles—one shuts out the sight of the candle-light while pronouncing the benediction, and immediately after completing the benediction one removes one's hands and gazes upon the light, which act is considered as if one said the benediction before kindling the light of the candles.

The benediction to be recited over the Sabbath candles is:

בָּרוּךְ אַתָּה יְהֹוָה אֱלֹהֵינוּ, מֶלֶךְ הָעוֹלָם, אֲשֶׁר קִדְּשָׁנוּ בְּמִצְוֹתָיו,
וְצִוָּנוּ לְהַדְלִיק נֵר שֶׁל שַׁבָּת.

"Barukh attah adonai, elohenu melekh haolam, asher kidshanu bemitzvotav, vetzivanu lehadlik ner shel shabbat."

"Praised be Thou, O Lord our God, King of the universe, who hast sanctified us by Thy commandments, and hast commanded us to light the Sabbath candles."

After lighting the Sabbath candles it is customary for the devoted mother to offer a special prayer for her family:

"Almighty God, Thou hast chosen the Sabbath-day as a day of rest and holy devotion, and commanded us to light candles in honor of that Holy Day. With joyful emotions did I light the Sabbath candles, in compliance with Thy precept, in order to honor and sanctify Thy great name, Thy holy Torah and the Sabbath.

"O Lord, how precious is the Day of Rest which Thou hast given us in Thine abundant kindness! Many are the cares and the sorrows of the week-days, and many are the struggles in life. But when the holy Sabbath appears, rest and peace enter our hearts; the restless desires and constant struggles for earthly gains which have prevailed during the week, give way, on the Sabbath, to sweet repose of mind, to pleasant and quieting emotions.

"God of Abraham, Isaac and Jacob, how can we sufficiently thank Thee for all Thy heavenly grace and goodness? Throughout the week, Thou didst surround us with Thy gracious protection and mercy. From day to day Thy heavenly blessings descended upon us. At the end of the week, which has been so full of Thy manifold gifts, Thou gavest us the choicest of all heavenly boons, the holy Sabbath Day, which pours soft, heavenly light upon our pilgrim path on earth.

"Bless, then, O my God, this holy Day of Rest, and grant us understanding that we may

more and more improve in the knowledge of
Thee, and thus be enabled to walk in Thy ways,
and become worthy of Thy benevolence. Grant
protection unto me and mine, and guard us
against sorrow, accident and evil occurrences on
this day of rest and repose. May the rays of
the Sabbath light, symbolic of Thy holiness,
illumine the week of toil and labor, and exalt
all our life's days.

"Merciful Father in heaven, aid us to con-
quer every temptation and allurement of sin,
and cause the light of joy to burn in our hearts,
and the light of love and peace to shine in our
homes.

"Grant, O Lord, that my children grow
up learned in Thy holy Torah, and may they
always be guided by its benign light that they
may at all times serve Thee with all their heart,
and soul, and might.

"May the words of my mouth and the
meditation of my heart be acceptable in Thy
sight, O Lord, my Rock and my Redeemer.
AMEN."

Remember that you may perform no work
whatsoever after you have lit the Sabbath
candles, because you have already assumed the
holiness of the Sabbath.

SABBATH EVE Especially on the holy day of Sabbath, it is essential that peace and harmony reign in the Jewish home. Our Rabbis say that the Sabbath can best be honored by peace and amiability. And you, Jewish woman, can become a virtual angel of peace, bringing happiness and sunshine in your home at all times.

Our Talmudic sages say that on Sabbath eve every man is escorted to his home by two ministering angels, sent down from heaven. One is dark with an evil somber face, and the other is gracious and beautiful. If the man's house is still in weekday disorder, the table undecked for the Sabbath meal, and the mistress of the house unfriendly and quarrelsome, the evil angel declares in triumph: "May the next Sabbath, in this house, be like this one;" to which the good angel is forced to murmur a sad "Amen." But if the house is spic and span, the Sabbath candles lighted, the table set for the Friday evening meal, and the mistress of the house friendly and kind, the good angel exclaims in delight: "May the next Sabbath, in this house, be enjoyed in equal fashion," and the bad angel is forced to respond "Amen."

Because the Jewish woman is the spirit and the life of the home, our sages decreed that the husband, on Friday evening, should recite proverbs, Chapter xxi, veress 10-30. In these beautiful poetic verses, King Solomon sings the praises of the valiant God-fearing Jewish woman whom the husband must love, cherish and admire above all earthly treasures.

KIDDUSH (SANCTIFICATION) Our Rabbis of old decreed that the Sabbath should be sanctified by reciting the *kiddush*, a prayer said over a goblet of wine at the coming of the Sabbath. In honor of this occasion, God-fearing Jews obtain the best wine they can afford.

Some Jewish families are unable to procure wine for the *kiddush,* and as no other beverage may be used for this purpose, they recite the *kiddush* over two whole *hallot,* white loaves of bread especially baked for the Sabbath, either by the mistress of the house herself, or by a baker. In some Jewish homes the mistress of the house bakes two small *hallot* for each and every male member of the family.

When the *kiddush* is recited over wine, the *hallot* must be covered, in order not to disgrace them.

The *kiddush* must be recited in the room where the evening meal is served.

According to the Jewish law, women, too, are obliged to say the *kiddush,* since they too must observe the holiness of the Sabbath. However, they can fulfill the duty of saying the *kiddush* by attentively listening to its recital by someone else, and by responding "Amen." It is, however, best that she repeat the *kiddush* silently as it is recited. Every one present should taste some of the wine over which the *kiddush* was recited, but without saying the benediction.

THE SABBATH MEALS After *kiddush,* the hands are washed and the appropriate benediction is pronounced. (See page 84). Then the master of the house breaks bread pronouncing the benediction *hamotzi* over it. (See page 84). If each member of the house is not provided with his own *hallot,* the master of the house distributes a slice of his own loaf to each member of the family who likewise recites the *hamotzi* over it.

Now, the meal, which consists of the best food the mistress of the house could afford to buy, is served. Stuffed fish has long been a favorite dish for this occasion, and there are many other Sabbath favorites. Between courses, pious Jews chant *zemirot,* special Sabbath hymns. Everybody merrily joins in the singing. The meal is concluded by the recital of Grace.

During the Sabbath-day every Jew, man or woman, must eat three meals, one on Sabbath eve, and two during the day.

THE HOLINESS OF THE SABBATH It is your sacred duty to keep the Sabbath holy, refraining from performing manual work and from going out shopping. If your husband is forced by circumstances to violate the Sabbath, still, it is your duty, as wife and mother, for the purpose of training and bringing up your children in a Jewish atmosphere, to do everything you can to keep the sanctity of the day.

If, however, there is any question of danger to human life, that life must be saved even if it means that the Sabbath must be violated.

There must be no mourning, weeping, or sadness on the Sabbath. It must be observed as a day of rest, joy and happiness.

SPIRITUAL DEVOTION The Day of Rest should be devoted to spiritual matters, because they afford happiness. Devote the Sabbath to forming a genuine intimacy with your children. Keep them about you, study them, and instill in them devotion to their God and to their people; acquaint them with the Jewish ideals and traditions. Your children will then look forward with pleasure to the arrival of the Sabbath.

It has been proven time and again, throughout the history of the human race, that you, with your keen understanding, intelligence, and profound love and devotion, can have a great influence over your husband and your family. You are therefore to be held accountable for their conduct. You can lead your husband as well as your children upon the path of righteousness and goodness. It lies within your power to mould their character.

HABDALAH   *Habdalah* is a term used for the ceremony and prayers by means of which a division is made between the Sabbath and work-day. The Jewish law requires that a formal separation be made between holy and profane times, and prohibits the resumption of ordinary work after the Sabbath or a festival until that division has been made. This is accomplished by performing the *habdalah* ceremony at the conclusion of the Sabbath or festival. This ceremony is performed over a cup of wine or any other beverage, except water. In the *habdalah* ceremony are included benedictions over spices and freshly kindled lights.

The *habdalah* ceremony must be observed by women as well as by men. Their duty may be fulfilled by listening to their husbands, or others, reciting the prayer and by responding "Amen." The pious Jewish woman bids the Sabbath farewell by reciting a beautiful prayer, in which she offers thanks to the Almighty for His gift, the Sabbath, and prays for the health and happiness of her own family as well as of all the people of Israel.

The Habdalah Prayer

"God of Abraham, Isaac and Jacob! With loving kindness dost Thou care for all the creatures which Thou in Thy wisdom hast created in this vast universe, providing them with all their needs and wants. Pray accept the prayer of Thy handmaid who now stands before Thee pouring out her soul in prayer and supplication.

"The Holy Sabbath is now departing, and with it goes all the divine bliss, rest and repose. A new week is beginning, bringing with it all tribulations, woes, and sorrows. In Thee alone, O Lord, is our hope and salvation.

"Grant, O Lord, that the new week now beginning be blessed with Thy goodness and prosperity. May it be a week of happiness and joy for Thy people Israel scattered in the four corners of the earth.

"Merciful Father! Open unto us the gates of knowledge and of understanding, that we may know to shun evil and sin and all that is immoral; and permit us to enter the gates of virtue, piety and chastity. Open unto us the gates of contentment and peace, of universal unity and brotherly love, that we may hate no one, and no one may hate us. Open unto us the gates of blessing, prosperity and happiness, that all our works may be crowned with success. Open unto us the gates of joy and delight, and let Thy heavenly light shine upon our ways. Open unto us the gates of good tidings and consolation, that Thy people Israel may be comforted by beholding the restoration of Thy Holy Temple in Jerusalem. O send us Thy prophet Elijah to announce the arrival of our redeemer, the Messiah, so that the long night of darkness, exile and misery may come to an end.

"Grant, O Lord, that all Jewish homes, including mine, enjoy the new week in good health, peace and contentment. Bless all children of Israel with Thy paternal blessing. AMEN."

THE THREE PILGRIM FESTIVALS

PASSOVER, FEAST OF UNLEAVENED BREAD

SHABUOT, FEAST OF WEEKS

SUKKOT, FEAST OF TABERNACLES

"Three times in a year shall all thy males appear before the Lord thy God in the place which He shall choose: on the Feast of Unleavened Bread, on the Feast of Weeks, and on the Feast of Tabernacles; and they shall not appear before the Lord empty; every man shall give as he is able, according to the blessing of the Lord thy God which he hath given thee."

(DEUTERONOMY XVI, 16-17).

NOTA KOSLOWSKY

THE THREE PILGRIM FESTIVALS :

PASSOVER, SHABUOT, AND SUKKOT

1. CONCERNING FESTIVALS IN GENERAL

THE TIME OF THE FEAST According to the law of Moses, on Passover and Sukkot only the first and the last days are to be observed as a strict festival on which no manual work may be performed. Shabuot and Rosh Hashanah, according to the biblical law, were to be observed for only one day each. However, the changing conditions of Jewish life before the fall of Jerusalem were responsible for the introduction of an extra day of the feast.

Until the middle of the fourth century, C. E., no calendar had yet been established, and the dates for the observance of the festivals were fixed by the Sanhedrin, the Supreme Court at Jerusalem. Because of the persecution of the Jews by the Roman Caesars, the decision of the Sanhedrin could not readily be conveyed to the distant Jewish settlements. The communities outside of Palestine were therefore instructed to add an extra day to each festival, to make certain that the festival would be observed on the proper day as required by the Law of God. Passover was then extended to eight days, instead of seven, and Sukkot to nine days instead of eight, the first two and the last two days of which were observed as a strict festival. Shabuot and Rosh Hashanah were given one additional day each.

In 360, C. E., Hillel II framed a permanent calendar, the principles of which hold good to this day, and fixed precisely the dates of the various holidays. The dates no longer being in doubt, the Rabbis of Babylonia wished to drop the extra day of the festivals, but they were advised by the Palestinian authorities not to break an established custom. Even today, therefore, orthodox Jewry observes this long established custom.

HONORING THE FESTIVAL It is the duty of every man and woman to honor the festival, by beginning it with a tidy appearance.

Before each festival, therefore, every Jewish woman should bathe in warm water, have her nails pared and her hair dressed. She must have her house cleaned especially for the occasion, put fresh linen on the beds, set the table with the best silverware and dishes, have the *hallot* on the table and a cup for the *kiddush*, and also the candlesticks for the lighting of the festival candles.

It is the duty of every Jewish woman to prepare sumptuous meals for the festival, and to honor it by lighting the candles and pronouncing the proper benedictions over them.

REJOICING ON THE FESTIVAL Because the word *rejoicing* is mentioned by the Lord our God in connection with festivals, the meals on such days should be more sumptuously prepared than on the Sabbath. The festival garments should also be costlier than those of the Sabbath. Not only must you yourself be happy and cheerful, but you are duty-bound to make everyone else feel happy by your kind attitude and demeanor.

But your own happiness and gaiety and that of your family does not yet constitute real Jewish happiness. Jews must share their happiness with those who are less fortunate than themselves. When they are about to enjoy good food and drink on the festival, they must not neglect the orphan, the widow and others who are in need. They must help provide them with food, drink, and clothes, so that they too may enjoy their festivals and be happy. To enjoy good food and drink on a festival together with one's family, and to refuse to help provide for the poor and those whose souls are embittered, is mere gluttony. To such gluttons our holy sages apply the biblical verse: "Their sacrifices shall be unto them as the bread of mourners; all that eat thereof shall be polluted; for their food is only for themselves."

No less than two meals must be served on each of the festival days, one at night and one during the day.

FESTIVAL CANDLES AND KIDDUSH The festival must be inaugurated by lighting the festival candles, and by reciting the *kiddush* (sanctification) over wine. Of this we shall treat later with references to each particular festival. However, it is necessary to state here one general rule of law applying to all festivals: The candles for the second day of a festival should not be lit before the appearance of the stars.

WHAT MAY AND MAY NOT BE DONE ON A FESTIVAL According to the Law of God, a festival must be observed as a day of rest and happiness. No manual labor may be performed on such a day. The only work permissible is that which is needed to supply food for human beings.

However, food may not be prepared on one day of the festival for use on another. Only food needed for that very day may be prepared.

Kneading dough is permissible on a festival, but one is not allowed to measure the flour or other ingredients. These must be taken by approximation. They may, however, be measured in the following manner: Put a quantity of the ingredient in a larger measure and then subtract from it whatever portion you do not need; or, place it in a smaller measure and then add to it as much as you need.

Hallah (see pages 107-111) may be taken from the dough kneaded on the festival, but it may not be burned on the festival. The dough separated for the *hallah* should be put in a safe place until after the conclusion of the festival when it should be burnt.

No *hallah* may be separated on a festival from dough that has been kneaded before the festival. But you may bake such dough and eat it, leaving a portion from which the *hallah* may be separated after the festival is over.

No light may be kindled on a festival which is not needed either for cooking, baking, heating or lighting the house. A Jahrzeit lamp (see page 330) may not be lit on a festival.

ERUB TABSHILIN As has been stated before, on a festival no food may be prepared from one day to the other. If, however, the two days of a festival occur either on Friday and Saturday or Thursday and Friday, and food must be prepared on one of the festival days for Saturday, then it is necessary to perform the ceremony of *erub tabshilin,* meaning *combination of dishes,* which sanctions the preparation of food on the festival for the Sabbath. The ceremony is performed as follows:

On the afternoon preceding the festival, before sundown, the master of the house takes a piece of bread together with some cooked or roasted food, which is generally eaten with bread, such as eggs, meat or fish, and pronounces the following benediction:

בָּרוּךְ אַתָּה יְהֹוָה אֱלֹהֵינוּ, מֶלֶךְ הָעוֹלָם, אֲשֶׁר קִדְּשָׁנוּ בְּמִצְוֹתָיו, וְצִוָּנוּ עַל מִצְוַת עֵרוּב.

"Barukh attah adonai, elohenu melekh haolam, asher kidshanu bemitzvotav, vetzivanu al mitzvat erub."

"Praised be Thou, O Lord our God, King of the universe, who hast sanctified us by Thy commandments, and hast commanded us concerning the observance of the *erub.*"

The following formula is then added: "By

virtue of this *erub* be it permitted us to bake, cook, keep the victuals warm, light the candles, and do all the work that is necessary on the festival for the Sabbath."

If a woman has no husband, she herself is required to perform the ceremony of *erub tabshilin.*

Only on Friday may food be prepared for the Sabbath by means of the *erub tabshilin* ceremony. If therefore the festival falls on Thursday and Friday, no food may be prepared on Thursday to be used on the Sabbath.

SPIRITUAL DEVOTION Although eating dainty food and drinking good wine on a festival is considered a *mitzvah,* a meritorious act, nevertheless a person ought not to spend the whole day in eating and drinking. According to the Talmudic sages, every Jew must devote half of the festival day to prayer, study of the Law, and other good deeds.

It is entirely up to you, the Jewish woman, to endow your house with a festival spirit. Be with your children, teach them, and know them.

HOL HAMOED The days intervening between the first two days and the last two days of a festival are known as *hol hamoed,* semi-holidays. Manual labor may be performed during *hol hamoed*, but certain kinds of work are forbidden.

No washing that might have been done before may be done during *hol hamoed*, even when needed for the festival. Infants' diapers may be washed during *hol hamoed*, because they are in constant need. However, all washing, even when allowable, must be done privately.

2. PASSOVER (PESAH)

THE FESTIVAL OF FREEDOM

WHAT IS PASSOVER? When our forefathers, in olden times, were held as slaves in Egypt, God sent two messengers, Moses and his brother Aaron, with a plea to the Egyptian ruler, known among his subjects as Pharaoh, to let His people go out of Pharaoh's land as free men. Pharaoh refused to listen to the word of God, and for this he and the Egyptian people were punished with ten plagues. The last of these plagues was the slaying of the first-born sons of the Egyptians. At midnight, the Angel of Death visited the homes of the Egyptians, killing their first-born sons, but he *passed over* the houses of the Israelites and spared their first-born. This festival therefore is called *Passover;* or, in Hebrew, *Pesah.*

THE FESTIVAL OF FREEDOM Passover is the Jewish festival of freedom. It commemorates the birth of a free nation, and the Almighty's deliverance of our forefathers from slavery in Egypt through His servant Moses.

Just after midnight, on the fourteenth day

of the Jewish month of Nisan, when the tenth
plague fell upon the Egyptians, Pharaoh drove
the Jews from the land. The Jewish women
had no time to bake the bread for which they
had prepared the dough. They had not even
time to allow the dough to be leavened. The
Jewish women took their dough before it was
leavened, and they carried their kneading-
troughs bound up in their clothes upon their
shoulders.

AN
AGRICULTURAL
FESTIVAL

The Passover festival is also the
agricultural spring holiday of
the Jewish people. It was celebrated in Palestine as the be-
ginning of harvest by our forefathers, who were
close to the soil.

In Palestine, the grain harvest lasted seven
weeks, and was observed by the Jews as a season of gladness and joy. This festive season
began with the harvest of barley on the second
day of Passover. No one had been permitted
to eat of the new crop of grain until this day
when a thanksgiving-offering was brought to
the Almighty, in gratitude for the products of
the soil which He had caused to grow. The
offering—called *omer* in Hebrew—was a measure
of the new barley flour which was the first

cereal to ripen. This offering was brought to the Temple at Jerusalem where it was presented to the priest, who waved it before the Almighty and offered thanks to Him. The grain harvest ended with the harvesting of wheat on the fiftieth day after the bringing of the *omer*, and this occasion was celebrated by the festival of Shabuot (Pentecost).

A PILGRIM FESTIVAL Passover was the first of the three great pilgrim festivals, when the people of Palestine from far and near, travelled in gala procession with their families to Jerusalem, the Holy City. The Jews made their pilgrimage before Passover, so that they might eat of the Paschal Lamb, the Passover-offering, in Jerusalem, near the Temple of God.

LEAVENED FOOD IS FORBIDDEN It is expressly forbidden to eat *hametz*, leavened food, during the eight days of Passover. Even pots, pans, china and silverware used throughout the year are considered *hametz*, and may not be used during Passover. Jewish housewives must thoroughly cleanse such utensils before Passover and put them away where they cannot be easily reached, in order to preclude the possibility of their being used through error during the Passover festival. It is advisable that they should keep in readiness, from year to year, a complete set of tablewear and kitchen utensils for use on the Passover.

Some utensils, used during the year, may be retained for Passover use after *kashering* them, that is, passing them through boiling water and fire. However, as the law concerning the ritual of *kashering* utensils is not known to everybody, it is advisable that before going through such process, a Rabbi conversant with the Jewish law should be consulted.

THE
SEARCH
FOR
LEAVEN
The Lord God commanded through Moses that the Jews abstain from eating *hametz* during the Passover week, and that they also remove all manner of leavened food from their domain, so that during the Passover week "no leaven shall be found in your houses."

Before the approach of Passover, preparations must be begun for the removal of leaven to comply with the Law of God. The Jewish housewife must see to it that her home is thoroughly cleansed from cellar to garret, so that on the thirteenth day of Nisan no trace of leavened food remains. Rooms and storehouses, where leaven might have been brought in throughout the year, must be carefully swept and cleansed on that day.

A formal search for leaven was instituted by our sages many centuries back. This search must take place on the thirteenth day of Nisan, on the evening before Passover, immediately after nightfall. If the first day of Passover occurs on a Sunday, the formal search must be made after nightfall on Thursday evening, the twelfth day of Nisan.

The search for leaven is carried out in the following manner: The master of the household, or another in his absence, puts away in a safe place all the *hametz* that has been left for food or for sale, and covers it up. He then deposits a few crumbs of bread in some noticeable place, generally on one of the window-sills in each room, takes a wooden spoon and a small brush, or a few whole feathers, and then lights a wax-taper or candle. Accompanied by another member of the household who carries the lit taper or candle, the performer of the ceremony makes a complete round of the house, searching every nook and corner, and examining the pockets of his own clothes and those of the clothes of his household, to be sure that no leaven is left there. While making the round, he gathers up all the leaven he can find. Coming to the window-

sills where the crumbs of bread have been de-
posited, he carefully sweeps the crumbs with
the brush or with the feathers into the wooden
spoon, leaving the crumbs on the sill.

When gathering up the crumbs from the
first window-sill, the searcher pronounces the
following benediction:

בָּרוּךְ אַתָּה יְהֹוָה אֱלֹהֵינוּ, מֶלֶךְ הָעוֹלָם, אֲשֶׁר קִדְּשָׁנוּ בְּמִצְוֹתָיו,
וְצִוָּנוּ עַל בִּעוּר חָמֵץ.

"Barukh attah adonai, elohenu melekh
haolam, asher kidshanu bemitzvotav, vetzivanu
al biur hametz."

"Praised be Thou, O Lord our God, King
of the universe, who hast sanctified us by Thy
commandments, and hast commanded us to
clean away the leaven."

Completing the search for leaven, the
searcher nullifies whatever *hametz* remains in
his possession, by resolving to consider it as non-
existent, entirely valueless and comparable to
dust, and as something for which he has no use.
He performs that resolution by reciting the special formula prescribed by the sages: "All manner of leaven that remains in my domain, which
I have not seen or removed, shall be considered
null and void, and accounted as the dust of the
earth."

The searcher takes whatever leaven he has found, together with the spoon and brush or feathers, and carefully ties them together. He puts it all away where it may easily be seen by him the following day.

BURNING HAMETZ On the fourteenth day of Nisan, the day preceding the Passover, before eleven o'clock in the morning, the master of the house-hold burns the leaven he has put away the evening before, together with the spoon and brush or feathers. If the first day of Passover occurs on a Sunday, the burning of the *hametz* must take place on Friday, the thirteenth day of Nisan.

After burning the leaven, he recites the following formula as ordained by the sages: "All manner of leaven remaining in my domain, whether it is visible to me or invisible, whether I have removed it or have failed to remove it, shall be considered null and void, and accounted as the dust of the earth."

A woman, too, is obligated by law to perform the ceremony of searching and burning *hametz* before Passover. However, a married woman whose husband is at home need not make the search, because her duty is fulfilled by her husband's going through such ceremony.

However, if her husband is away from home, she must go through the ceremony herself.

SELLING HAMETZ Any manner of leavened food, remaining after eleven o'clock in the forenoon before the Passover, the time limit set for burning of *hametz*, can neither be eaten nor sold to a non-Jew at any time; and at no time may anyone derive benefit from it. If therefore a person has leavened food in his possession which he does not wish to destroy or burn, and he wants to derive benefit from it after Passover, he must sell it to a non-Jew before eleven o'clock, the morning of the day before Passover. As not everybody is familiar with the law regulating such sale and therefore is not in a position to comply with the legal requirements, the custom prevails to sell the leaven to the Rabbi of the community, who, as agent, sells it in turn to a non-Jew.

MATZAH The *matzah*, unleavened bread, which the Jews eat during the Passover week, is known in Jewish literature as the bread of affliction. It is reminiscent of the hardships of our forefathers in Egypt. *Matzah* has no special flavor, as it contains no salt and no yeast. The dough for baking *matzah* must not be allowed to become leaven. For this reason, while kneading the dough, special percautions are taken against fermentation. It must be kneaded quickly, rolled into shape. and then perforated to keep the *matzah* from rising and swelling in baking.

Matzah is also symbolic of the haste with which our forefathers departed from Egypt, the land of their woe, that midnight when Pharaoh drove them without bread from the land, forcing them to take the dough which they carried with them wrapped in bundles.

WHEN MATZAH MUST BE EATEN While one is forbidden to eat leaven food, the eating of *matzah* is not compulsory during the eight days of Passover. One may eat any other food that one perfers, provided it is not classed as leaven.

On the first two nights of Passover, however, the eating of *matzah* is compulsory. Everyone, man or woman, must eat some *matzah* during the evening meal.

Before eating the *matzah* on these two

nights, the following two benedictions are pro-
nonuced:

בָּרוּךְ אַתָּה יְהֹוָה אֱלֹהֵינוּ, מֶלֶךְ הָעוֹלָם, הַמּוֹצִיא לָחֶם מִן הָאָרֶץ.

"Barukh attah adonai, elohenu melekh
haolam, hamotzi lehem min haaretz."

"Praised be Thou, O Lord our God, King
of the universe, who bringest forth bread from
the earth."

בָּרוּךְ אַתָּה יְהֹוָה אֱלֹהֵינוּ, מֶלֶךְ הָעוֹלָם, אֲשֶׁר קִדְּשָׁנוּ בְּמִצְוֹתָיו,
וְצִוָּנוּ עַל אֲכִילַת מַצָּה.

"Barukh attah adonai, elohenu melekh
haolam, asher kidshanu bemitzvotav, vetzivanu
al akhilat matzah."

"Praised be Thou, O Lord our God, King
of the universe, who hast sanctified us by Thy
commandments, and hast commanded us to eat
matzah."

THE MATZAH FUND At the approach of any festival, the
first duty of every Jew is to give
thought to persons in need, to those
less fortunate than himself. If a Jew
fails to provide for the needy, but enjoys the

[156]

festival meals with his wife and children behind locked doors, he is not fulfilling the will of the Merciful One in the observance of His festivals.

In every Jewish community, therefore, there has been handed down, from time immemorial, the beautiful custom for every Jew to donate, according to his means, toward a *matzah fund*, known as *maot ḥiṭṭim*, literally, *money for wheat*. The object of this fund is to provide every poor Jewish family with *matzah* and with all other things necessary for the enjoyment of the festival. It was called *money for wheat*, because in former years the head of every Jewish family used to purchase for himself a supply of wheat suitable for Passover; he would bring the wheat to a mill, which had been cleansed and prepared for Passover use, where it would be ground into flour. He would then take the flour to a bakery specially fitted out for the baking of the *matzah*.

MATZAH AND LEAVEN BEFORE PASSOVER On the day before Passover all Jews abstain from eating leavened food after one-third of the day has passed; that is, one-third of the time between dawn and the appearance of the stars, usually about ten o'clock in the morning. They likewise abstain from eating *matzah* during the entire day before Passover, so that the *matzah* may be eaten with relish at night when everybody is duty-bound to eat it and pronounce a benediction over it.

THE SEDER NIGHTS On the first two nights of Passover, the *seder* is celebrated in the Jewish home. *Seder* is the special order or program designated for these two nights. No other ceremony among Jews is celebrated with such pomp and gladness of heart as the *seder*. This interesting ceremony was originally designed to stimulate the interest of the Jewish child in the glorious past of his people, and to inspire him with hope for the future. When a child asks, upon seeing the special order of things on *seder* night, "what is the meaning of all this?" he is told in explanation, the story of his people's deliverance from the Egyptian bondage. And, by reciting the *Haggadah*, the special book adopted for the *Seder* nights, the entire family, man, woman and child, are imbued with a spirit of loyalty to their God and their people. They are encouraged by an unswerving faith in their God to face the trials of their long dark exile. As their fathers, they say, were helped in time of darkness and persecution, so will they, too, survive their tormentors, until at last the true Messiah will bring an era of freedom, justice and good-will to men.

THE FOUR
CUPS OF
WINE

In the afternoon of the fourteenth day of Nisan, the Jewish housewife, assisted by all members of the family, begins setting the table for the *seder*, spreading it with the best linen in her possession, and decorating it with the family's best china and silverware, specially kept from year to year for the Passover. One goblet or wine-glass is placed on the table for each and every one who is to participate in the *seder* service. Every participant, whether male or female, must, during the course of the *seder* service, drink exactly four cups of wine, mead, or grape-juice as a symbol of the four biblical expressions used by the Almighty in promising the Jews redemption from the Egyptian bondage.

THE CUP
OF ELIJAH

In addition to the cups or glasses set on the table for each participant in the celebration, there developed the custom of placing an extra large brimming cup of wine in the center of the table for the prophet Elijah.

This prophet, who was taken up to heaven alive in a fiery chariot drawn by fiery horses, is believed to have become immortal and to have become the heavenly guardian angel of the Jewish people. Elijah as the great champion of righteousness and of pure worship of God, at times, brings good fortune to poor people. It is he who is present at the celebration of every circumcision; and it is he who will appear in the end of days, to announce the arrival of the Messiah. At that time, this messenger of God will announce the good tidings, to the dwellers of the earth, of peace and salvation, of comfort to the sorrowing, of the resurrection of the dead, and of the establishment of the Divine Kingdom upon the earth.

On Passover night, at the celebration of the Feast of Liberty, the Jews invite Elijah to their homes, thereby indicating their implicit faith in the Almighty that some day He will send this immortal prophet to announce their deliverance from the hands of the modern Pharaohs. This also gave rise to the custom of opening the door during some stage of the *seder* service, in order that the long expected messenger, proclaiming the final redemption of mankind from all oppression, might enter the house as a most welcome guest.

THE SEDER PLATTER There is placed before the person conducting the *seder* ceremony, a large platter on which are to be found the following *seder* symbols: Three whole *matzot* each wrapped separately in a special cover or napkin, to represent the three divisions of Israel—Priests, Levites and laymen; a roasted shank-bone, placed on the right, symbolizing the Paschal lamb which was offered when the Temple was in existence; on the left, a roasted egg which represents the free-will offering, *haggigah*, which was presented on each day of the Feast during the existence of the Temple in Jerusalem; in the center, bitter herbs (horse-radish), symbolic of the bitterness of the Egyptian bondage; underneath the shank-bone, the dish of *haroseth*, a paste-like mixture of nuts, apples, cinnamon and raisins, finely chopped and mixed with wine, which in appearance resembles mortar, is symbolic of the hard construction labor of the Jews in Egypt; and parsley or watercress placed underneath the egg. In addition, parsley, watercress or lettuce and a dish of salt water are set upon the table for the whole company.

[161]

A POSITION
OF
FREEDOM
An improvised couch, generally consisting of a few cushions placed on the left side of an arm-chair, is provided for the person conduct-ing the *seder* ceremony. According to the Oriental custom, the position assumed by free men is one of reclining on the left side while eating. As a sign of freedom from the Egyptian bondage, it is customary for the person conduct-ing the ceremonies, to follow the precedent of the Orient.

LIGHTING
OF THE
FESTIVAL
CANDLES
All these preparations having been made, the mistress of the house sym-bolizes the joy which the festival brings into the Jewish home, by kindl-ing the festival candles. On both *seder* nights, the following two benedictions are recited over the candles:

(On Sabbath add the words in brackets)

בָּרוּךְ אַתָּה יְהוָֹה אֱלֹהֵינוּ, מֶלֶךְ הָעוֹלָם, אֲשֶׁר קִדְּשָׁנוּ בְּמִצְוֹתָיו,
וְצִוָּנוּ לְהַדְלִיק נֵר שֶׁל (שַׁבָּת וְשֶׁל) יוֹם טוֹב.

"Barukh attah adonai, elohenu melekh haolam, asher kidshanu bemitzvotav, vetzivanu lehadlik ner shel [shabbat veshel] yom tob."

"Praised be Thou, O Lord our God, King of the universe, who hast sanctified us by com-

maadments, and hast commanded us to light
the [Sabbath and the] festival candles."

בָּרוּךְ אַתָּה יְהֹוָה אֱלֹהֵינוּ, מֶלֶךְ הָעוֹלָם, שֶׁהֶחֱיָנוּ וְקִיְּמָנוּ, וְהִגִּיעָנוּ
לַזְּמַן הַזֶּה.

"Barukh attah adonai, elohenu melekh
haolam, sheheheyanu, vekiyemanu vehigianu
lazman hazzeh."

"Praised be Thou, O Lord our God, King
of the universe, who hast granted us life, sustained us and permitted us to reach this festive
season."

Then the following prayer may be added:

"O merciful Father, we thank Thee for
Thy loving kindness and never-ending goodness
to the house of Israel. Our ancestors languished
in Egyptian slavery; they ate the bread of affliction; the lash of the taskmaster drove them to
their labor; but Thou wast mindful of the children of Abraham, Isaac, and Jacob Thy faithful
servants. Thou didst raise up a deliverer, Moses,
who in Thy name brought the message of redemption to the enslaved. Thou didst lead Israel
from bondage to freedom, from darkness to light,
from despair to hope. As on eagle's pinions
Thou didst bear the children of Israel and bring
them unto Thee. From beneath the yoke of
oppression and ignorance Thou didst redeem

Israel to be unto Thee a kingdom of priests and a holy people. And in thankful memory of Thy wondrous deliverance, I lit these candles to celebrate the joyous feast of Passover.

"Ofttimes since that early day have we, the children of Israel, been oppressed; we have passed through more than one Egypt; hatred and prejudice laid a heavy yoke upon our necks. But through the darkness of misery and cruel oppression a ray of Thy grace continually shone above us. We never lost hope in Thee, O God, and our faith in Thee was ever firm. Nor was our trust misplaced. Ever and again Thy protecting love manifested itself, and we were saved from impending destruction.

"Our Father in heaven, we pray unto Thee on this day of our feast that, as Thou hast granted us Thy protection throughout the past, so mayest Thou be with us now and in the future. Deliver us from the oppressor's yoke. May all persecution cease and all traces of bondage disappear from among men. May we be worthy to behold the redemption when Thou wilt, in Thy great mercy, gather our people from the four corners of the earth and bring them back to Thy Holy Land. AMEN."

KIDDUSH (SANCTIFICATION) The *seder* ceremony is begun by filling all cups or wineglasses with wine—always a token of festivity among the Jews—and the master of the house recites over his wine the *kiddush*, the sanctification of the festival. All participants then drink from their cups, but before doing so, they recite the appropriate benediction either over wine or any other beverage that may be used instead. (For the benediction, see pages 86-87).

This is the first of the four cups of wine to be drunk during the *seder* ceremony. Mead, unfermented raisin-wine, or grape-juice may be used instead of wine by the womenfolk and children.

The *seder* ceremony is then followed as prescribed in the *Haggadah*.

THE DAYS OF REST The first two days of Passover, as commanded by the Lord God, must be kept and observed as holy. No work may be done on these two days, and all Jews must enjoy rest, peace and happiness. Only food needed for human beings may be prepared and cooked on a festival. (For a full explana-

tion of the laws concerning festivals, see pages
142-143).

HOL
HAMOED

After the first two days of Passover
follow four days of *hol hamoed* (semi
holidays). (As to the laws concerning *hol hamoed*, see page 145).

THE LAST
TWO DAYS

On the seventh day, after the departure of the Jews from the land
of Egypt, the Almighty performed
for the Jews the great miracle of dividing the
Red Sea. The redeemed Jews were saved from
destruction at the hand of Pharaoh's mighty
army, for all the Egyptians and their horses and
chariots who pursued them were drowned in
the Red Sea.

For the above reason, the Almighty commanded the Jews to observe this day as holy,
on which no manner of work may be done. (As
to the reason why an eighth day had been added
to Passover, see page 139).

Only one benediction is to be recited when
the festival candles are lit on the last two
days of Passover.

(On Sabbath add the words in brackets)

בָּרוּךְ אַתָּה יְהֹוָה אֱלֹהֵינוּ, מֶלֶךְ הָעוֹלָם, אֲשֶׁר קִדְּשָׁנוּ בְּמִצְוֹתָיו,
וְצִוָּנוּ לְהַדְלִיק נֵר שֶׁל ‹שַׁבָּת וְשֶׁל› יוֹם טוֹב.

"Barukh attah adonai, elohenu melekh haolam, asher kidshanu bemitzvotav, vetzivanu lehadlik ner shel [shabbat veshel] yom tob."

"Praised be Thou, O Lord our God, King of the universe, who hast sanctified us by Thy commandments, and hast commanded us to kindle the [Sabbath and the] festival candles."

On the eighth day of Passover, Memorial Services, *yizkor* (1), are held for the departed, at the synagogue. If one is unable to attend the synagogue services, one should recite the Memorial Services at home. (For the order of Memorial Services and the Yizkor Calendar, see pages 334-341).

It is not permitted to eat any leavened food on the eighth day of Passover before the appearance of the stars. Pious Jews abstain from eating bread baked in Jewish bakeries during the Passover festival.

(1) A **yizkor** calendar for twenty years, on page 341.

3. SHABUOT (PENTECOST)

FEAST OF WEEKS

WHAT IS SHABUOT? The holiday Shabuot—the Hebrew word for weeks — takes its name from the date of celebration: exactly seven weeks after the second day of Passover, which corresponds to the sixth day of the Jewish month of Sivan. The Shabuot festival is commonly known as Pentecost, which in Greek means fiftieth day, because it is celebrated on the fiftieth day counting from the second day of Passover.

The Shabuot festival is holy to God. He therefore commanded that all Jews must observe it as a strict holiday, by resting and refraining from all manner of work, and He likewise ordered that it should be celebrated with merriment and joy.

AN AGRICULTURAL FESTIVAL It has been noted in connection with the Passover celebration, that when the Jews were in Palestine and were closely bound to the soil, they observed their harvest seasons as holidays. It was on the second day of Passover that the cereal harvest began in Palestine, an event which was celebrated by bringing the *omer* offering of barley which was the first cereal to ripen. The harvest celebration ended with the harvesting of wheat on Shabuot, the wheat being the last cereal to ripen. The celebration of Shabuot thus marked the conclusion of the cereal harvest.

On Shabuot, during the existence of the Temple at Jerusalem, the whole Jewish community brought a thanksgiving offering to the Almighty. This consisted of two loaves of bread baked of fine flour from the new crop of wheat, which were waved by the priest before the Lord. The sacrifice was accompanied by the Levites' singing of hymns and the playing of harps and other musical instruments.

Shabuot was celebrated also as the festival of the first ripe fruit, or, as it is known in Hebrew, *hag habikkurim*. The fruit harvest commenced on Shabuot and ended on Sukkot in the Fall. Every farmer had to bring his first ripe fruit to the Temple at Jerusalem where he gave thanks to the Almighty for the products of his field.

THE
PILGRIMAGE
TO
JERUSALEM
Shabuot was the second of the three great pilgrim feasts, when the people of Palestine, from far and near, travelled with their families in gala procession to the Holy City to be near the Temple of God. Before the feast of Shabuot, every farmer, no matter how poor or rich he may have been, put his first ripe fruit in a basket made of gold or of silver, or of wicker-work, and presented it to the priest.

The procession of the pilgrims with their *bikkurim*, as described in the Mishnah, was very impressive:

The people came from the villages and colonies to the chief town of each district. There they spent the night in open squares, without going into the houses (probably to attract the attention of the people). At dawn they were awakened by the officer in charge with the call: "Arise, let us ascend to Zion, the house of the Lord our God."

Those who lived near Jerusalem brought fresh figs and grapes, while those that came from distant parts brought dried figs and raisins. The bull destined for the sacrifice, his horns guilded and his head wreathed with olive leaves, led the procession. To the playing of a flute, the pilgrims marched to the gates of Jerusalem. There they were met by the Temple officers and by many artisans, who greeted them, saying: "Our brethren from (this or that town), enter the city in peace."

With the flute still playing, the pilgrims proceeded to the Temple-court. All pilgrims, including the king, now carried their baskets on their shoulders to the outer court of the Temple, where they were welcomed by the Levites, singing: "I will extol Thee, O Lord, for Thou hast raised me up, and Thou hast not suffered mine enemies to rejoice over me." Doves, which had been carried by the pilgrims in their baskets, were sacrificed as burn-offerings on the altar.

With his basket on his shoulder, the pilgrim recited from the Holy Scriptures a part of the prescribed prayer. He then lowered his basket from his shoulder, and a priest placed his hands beneath the basket and raised it as a thanksgiving offering, and continued to read to the end of the biblical prayer. The pilgrim then placed the basket with the first ripe fruit near the altar, bowed down, and left the hall.

IN MODERN PALESTINE Like their ancestors of antiquity, many Jews now living in Palestine are engaged in farming. With great joy and renewed hope they, too, celebrate the end of the cereal harvest. But they do not give their *bikkurim* to the priest, as was done in olden times; instead, they give it to a national fund, called *keren kayyemet*, founded for the purpose of purchasing more land in Palestine in which to settle more pioneers. Neither do the Jews celebrate the *bikkurim* feast only in Jerusalem, as their forefathers had done, but they hold celebrations in many places.

A TORAH FESTIVAL The festival of Shabuot has an additional meaning. On this day God revealed Himself on Mount Sinai and gave the Israelites the Ten Commandments. For this reason the Rabbis declared Shabuot as the most enjoyable of all Jewish holidays.

CUSTOMS OBSERVED ON SHABUOT A popular custom on Shabuot is to eat dairy food and cheese-cakes and blintzes (fritters stuffed with cheese), and to serve honey with the meals. This custom has developed in honor of the Law of God, which is likened to "honey and milk." The meat meal follows the dairy meal, because no Jewish festival is complete without serving meat. These two meals represent the two loaves of bread which in ancient times were used in the *bikkurim* offering.

On Shabuot it is customary to cover the floors with greens and to decorate the house and the synagogue with plants, flowers and even with trees. The greens serve to remind one of the green mountains of Sinai; they also commemorate the harvest festival of former times.

Because the Jewish people received the Law of God on Shabuot and were thus confirmed in the covenant, the beautiful custom of confirmation has been introduced in some of our modern synagogues. Boys and girls, who have been prepared in Hebrew or Sunday Schools, attend the morning service at the synagogue and are confirmed in the Jewish faith as our forefathers were on this day. It is a great event for the school children as well as for their parents and friends.

THE FESTIVAL CANDLES The festival candles must be lit on the first and second nights of Shabuot, pronouncing the following two benedictions over them:

(On Sabbath add the words in brackets)

בָּרוּךְ אַתָּה יְהֹוָה אֱלֹהֵינוּ, מֶלֶךְ הָעוֹלָם, אֲשֶׁר קִדְּשָׁנוּ בְּמִצְוֹתָיו,
וְצִוָּנוּ לְהַדְלִיק נֵר שֶׁל (שַׁבָּת וְשֶׁל) יוֹם טוֹב.

"Barukh attah adonai, elohenu melekh haolam, asher kidshanu bemitzvotav, vetzivanu lehadlik ner shel [shabbat veshel] yom tob."

[173]

"Praised be Thou, O Lord our God, King of the universe, who hast sanctified us by Thy commandments, and hast commanded us to light [the Sabbath and] the festival candles."

בָּרוּךְ אַתָּה יְהֹוָה אֱלֹהֵינוּ, מֶלֶךְ הָעוֹלָם, שֶׁהֶחֱיָנוּ וְקִיְּמָנוּ, וְהִגִּיעָנוּ לִזְמַן הַזֶּה.

"Barukh attah adonai, elohenu melekh haolam, sheheheyanu, vekiyemanu, vehigianu lazman hazzeh."

"Praised be Thou, O Lord our God, King of the universe, who hast granted us life, sustained us and permitted us to reach this festive season."

Then the following prayer may be added:

"O Lord God, with a joyous heart and soul did I light the candles on this festival, on which Thou, in Thy graciousness, hast given unto our fathers on Sinai Thy holy Torah which is called LIGHT. Just as Thy holy Law, O God, has dispelled darkness from the peoples of the earth, so may the light of these candles dispel darkness and banish gloom from all houses of Thy people Israel.

"Merciful Father, Thou hast seen fit to choose the children of Israel to receive Thy Law, and through Thy servant Moses Thou didst reveal Thyself on Mount Sinai and didst give them

[174]

the Ten Commandments. With Thy Law in their hearts, Thy people wandered continually amidst deadly foes and devouring flames. But throughout the years, Thy people have been faithful to Thee. They found strength in trouble, light in darkness, and hope in despair, for they remembered Thy promise: 'I, the Lord, change not, and ye, O sons of Jacob, are not consumed.'

"May it be Thy will, O Lord our God, that the covenant made by our fathers at the foot of Sinai forever be a covenant of life and peace sealed in our hearts. Grant that Thy spirit, which was upon our fathers at Thy revelation, may not depart from us and from our children and from our children's children for ever.

"May the time not be distant, O Lord, when all the children of the earth shall worship Thy great name, when they shall abandon their superstitious beliefs and acknowledge Thy unity and Thy kingdom, and shall recognize Thee as their only God and Father. May the great day soon come, on which all nations shall go up to Thy holy mountain Zion, when Thy Temple at Jerusalem shall be a house of prayer for all nations and tongues, and from one end of the earth to the other the exulting shout shall be

heard: Zion, thy God reigneth, now and forever more! AMEN."

MEMORIAL SERVICES On the second day of Shabuot, Memorial Services (Yizkor) for the departed are said in the synagogue during the morning service. Those unable to attend the service at the synagogue, should re-cite the Memorial Prayers at home. (For the Memorial Service, and the Yizkor calendar see pages 334-341).

4. SUKKOT

WHAT IS SUKKOT? The feast of *Sukkot* (booths) is commemorative of the pioneer days of the Jewish People. When our ancestors in ancient times left Egypt, they wandered for forty years in the wilderness, before they were allowed to come to the promised land, pitching tents or building booths wherever they stopped. The Almighty, therefore, commanded that the Jewish people, throughout all generations, should celebrate the Feast of Tabernacles, or booths. For seven days, from the fifteenth to the twenty-second day of the month of Tishri, four days after Yom Kippur, they are to dwell in booths (*sukkot*).

THE SUKKAH The *sukkah* (*booth*) is a little tabernacle built of wood or canvas, and is covered with branches of trees and plants so that the heavens and the stars are visible over head. As this festival also commemorates the fruit harvest in Palestine, the interior of the *Sukkah* is decorated with flowers, and ripe fruits are suspended from the ceiling of leaves and branches.

[177]

During the festival, the *sukkah* is considered as one's temporary residence, and all meals must be served there. Some pious Jews even sleep there overnight.

According to Jewish law, a woman is not obliged to fulfill the precept of eating and drinking in the *sukkah*. But if she wishes to do so, it is considered praiseworthy, in which case she is to pronounce the benediction connected with the fulfillment of the precept:

בָּרוּךְ אַתָּה יְהוָֹה אֱלֹהֵינוּ, מֶלֶךְ הָעוֹלָם, אֲשֶׁר קִדְּשָׁנוּ בְּמִצְוֹתָיו,
וְצִוָּנוּ לֵישֵׁב בַּסֻּכָּה.

"Barukh attah adonai, elohenu melekh haolam, asher kidshanu bemitzvotav, vetzivanu lesheb basukkah."

"Praised be Thou, O Lord our God, King of the universe, who hast sanctified us by Thy commandments, and hast commanded us to dwell in the *sukkah*."

Train your children to learn to fulfill their duty to their God and to their people. Teach them, while they are young, to become a part of Jewish life and to cherish our great traditions. Teach them, if possible, to assist you in building the *sukkah* and in making it attractive and pleasant.

Minors are exempt from fulfilling the pre-

cept of dwelling in the *sukkah*. Yet it is praiseworthy to train children over five years of age in
the fulfillment of God's commandments.

The *sukkah* must be maintained with honor
and respect. After meals, the dishes should be
removed from the *sukkah* and washed elsewhere.
No menial work may be performed in the *sukkah*.

**THE
FESTIVAL
CANDLES** It is the duty of every Jewish woman
to try to the most of her ability to
brighten and decorate the *sukkah*. She
should bring into it the *hallot*, festival white breads shaped like a ladder, which
she has baked or bought especially for the occasion. She should bring along the candle-sticks
and the candles, and there light the festival
candles, pronouncing the following two benedictions:

(On Sabbath add the words included in
brackets)

בָּרוּךְ אַתָּה יְהֹוָה אֱלֹהֵינוּ, מֶלֶךְ הָעוֹלָם, אֲשֶׁר קִדְּשָׁנוּ בְּמִצְוֹתָיו,
וְצִוָּנוּ לְהַדְלִיק נֵר שֶׁל (שַׁבָּת וְשֶׁל) יוֹם טוֹב.

"Barukh attah adonai elohenu melekh
haolam, asher kidshanu bemitzvotav, vetzivanu
lehadlik ner shel [shabbat veshel] yom tob."

"Praised be Thou, O Lord our God, King

[179]

of the universe, who hast sanctified us by Thy commandments, and hast commanded us to light the [Sabbath and the] festival candles."

בָּרוּךְ אַתָּה יְהֹוָה אֱלֹהֵינוּ, מֶלֶךְ הָעוֹלָם, שֶׁהֶחֱיָנוּ וְקִיְּמָנוּ, וְהִגִּיעָנוּ לַזְּמַן הַזֶּה.

"Barukh attah adonai elohenu melekh haolam, sheheheyanu, vekiyemanu, vehigianu, lazman hazzeh."

"Praised be Thou, O Lord our God, King of the universe, who hast granted us life, sustained us, and permitted us to reach this festive season."

It is also customary to recite a special prayer after lighting the festival candles:

"I greatly rejoice, O Lord God, in fulfilling Thy holy command, which Thou in Thy mercy hast entrusted to the Jewish woman, to beautify and make holy the Feast of Tabernacles by lighting the festive candles.

"On this festival, we gratefully recall the loving care with which Thou didst watch over our fathers in the great wilderness. In their journey through the blighting desert, the wanderers found shelter from the scourching heat and beating tempest in the booth of Thy protecting love. In drought Thou didst refresh them with sprouting water from the rocks, and in famine

Thou didst preserve them by sending Manna from above for their nourishment. With a father's love Thou didst guide and shield them that they should become the bearers of Thy truth, and the champions of Thy Law.

"And as we greatfully recall the benefits Thou hast bestowed upon our forefathers in the wilderness, we pray unto Thee to graciously accept the thanks-offerings which we bring unto Thee on this day. In Thy goodness and mercy Thou hast enriched the earth with beauty and plenty, and hast provided abundantly for our needs. In field and in meadow, on hill-top and in valley, we witness the unceasing flow of Thy bounty. Thou hast surrounded us with the endless wonders of Thy creation and hast caused the light of Thy glory to shine into our hearts, that we may become ennobled by Thy spirit and may seek to glorify Thy holy name in all our ways.

"All-merciful God! Thy grace is without end, Thy mercy never ceases; every day, every hour is full of Thy loving-kindness; Thou blessest the fruit of our labors and providest all our needs. Withersoever we turn our eyes, we behold the shining testimonies of Thy mercy, filling us with joy and exultation. Yea, our souls hope in Thee. Our hearts rejoice in Thee,

and we confide in Thy holy name. O God, let
Thy mercy ever be with us, as we hope in Thee,
now and evermore. AMEN."

**AN
AGRICULTURAL
FESTIVAL**
Sukkot was really a festival of
thanksgiving. The agricultural
year was over at this time, particularly the fruit harvest. The
grapes were made into wine, and the olives
pressed into oil. All the other products of the
soil had been gathered, and the Palestinian Jews,
who were closely attached to the soil, celebrated
the event with merriment and festivity, and
rendered thanks to the Lord for the prosperous
season.

**THE FOUR
SPECIES**
To show their appreciation for the
Lord's bounty, the Jews were commanded to take four things — the
etrog (citron), the *lulab* (branch of a palm-
tree), myrtle branches, and willows of the brook
—and "rejoice before the Lord their God for
seven days," when celebrating the harvest festival.

Every morning, during the first seven
days of *sukkot*, except on the Sabbath, before
eating or drinking, the Jews take these four
things, and recite:

בָּרוּךְ אַתָּה יְהֹוָה אֱלֹהֵינוּ, מֶלֶךְ הָעוֹלָם, אֲשֶׁר קִדְּשָׁנוּ בְּמִצְוֹתָיו, וְצִוָּנוּ עַל נְטִילַת לוּלָב.

"Barukh attah adonai elohenu melekh haolam, asher kidshanu bemitzvotav, vetzivanu al netilat lulab."

"Praised be Thou, O Lord our God, King of the universe, who hast sanctified us by Thy commandments, and hast commanded us to take the *lulab*."

On the first day of *Sukkot* — if the first day falls on a Sabbath when the four species are not to be taken, then on the second day of *Sukkot*—the following benediction is added:

בָּרוּךְ אַתָּה יְהֹוָה אֱלֹהֵינוּ, מֶלֶךְ הָעוֹלָם, שֶׁהֶחֱיָנוּ וְקִיְּמָנוּ, וְהִגִּיעָנוּ לַזְּמַן הַזֶּה.

"Barukh attah adonai elohenu melekh haolam, sheheheyanu, vekiyemanu, vehigianu lazman hazzeh."

"Praised be Thou, O Lord our God, King of the universe, who hast granted us life, sustained us, and permitted us to reach this festive season."

The benediction over the *lulab* must be recited while standing. Before saying the benediction, the *lulab* should be taken in the right hand and the *etrog* in the left with the peduncle (the end that was attached to the stalk) upward and the end where the flower grew downward. As soon as the benediction is concluded, the *etrog* should be reversed with the peduncle downward, and holding the *etrog* close to the *lulab* (so as to make it appear one unit), they should be waved together slightly so that the *lulab* rustles.

In the synagogue, every morning when special prayers are recited, people possessing the *lulab* march through the aisles, led by the *hazzan* (cantor) who chants the prayers.

A PILGRIM'S FESTIVAL *Sukkot* was the last of the three festivals on which pilgrims from all over Palestine, and—during the existence of the second Temple—from neighboring lands as well marched into the Holy City, Jerusalem, to celebrate the Festival of Thanksgiving. This festival was designated by our Lord God as the *season of rejoicing*. Jerusalem was at this festival crowded with happy pilgrims, rejoicing before the Lord by offering sacrifices and joining the gay processions and ceremonies in the Temple, while the Levites played harps and other musical instruments.

REST DAYS The first two days of *Sukkot* are to be kept as strict holidays in accordance with the command of our Lord God, and no manual labor may be performed. Only the necessary preparation of food for human beings may be done. (See pages 142-143).

These two days of strict holiday are followed by five days of *hol hamoed*, semi holidays. (See page 145). The fifth day of *hol hamoed* is known as *Hoshanah Rabbah*, literally meaning *great help*. During the seven days of *Sukkot*, a special prayer was read daily at the morning service, called *hoshanot*, because they begin with the word *hoshanah* (pray, save). On this day the *hoshanot* are much longer than on the other days. This day is considered as somewhat holier than the other days of *hol hamoed*. This is due to the tradition that the season of judgment, which began with Rosh Hashanah, ends on Hoshanah Rabbah.

The meal served on Hoshanah Rabbah resembles the meal served at noon on the day before Yom Kippur. *Kreplach* (three-cornered fritters, stuffed with minced meat) is a favorite dish.

Little willow branches, also called *hoshanot*, are held and beaten during the morning service at the synagogue. This commemorates that during the existence of the Temple, a solemn procession of people carrying large branches walked around the altar on this day.

SHEMINI
ATZERET
The eighth day of *Sukkot* is called *shemini Atzeret,* (the eighth day of convocation). No work may be done on this day, and all laws pertaining to the observation of festivals must be observed on *Shemini Atzeret.* (See pages 142-143).

When the festival candles are lit on this day, the two benedictions, recited on the first two days of *Sukkot,* must be repeated. (See pages 179-180).

After lighting the festival candles, the following special prayer is read:

"Heavenly Father, I am deeply grateful to Thee for Thy loving kindness in that Thou hast spared me life and health to reach this Holy Day and to adorn it with the lighting of candles. May it be Thy will, O Lord, that Thou grantest us to enjoy other festivals in happiness and joy.

"Throughout this festive season, we have extolled Thee for the generous gifts of the earth. And on this day of *Shemini Atzeret,* we delight to render once more unto Thee our homage of thanksgiving and joyful praise. We lift up our hearts to Thee and extoll Thee for the blessings wherewith Thou crownest our days. Truly, O Lord, Thou art good to all, and Thy tender mercies are over all Thy works.

"Almighty God, grant that this pure festival joy may diffuse its blessings upon our future life. When this festival shall be concluded, and with it all the solemn days which we have spent in prayer and devotion, may we then carry with us into life all the pure and holy feelings which sanctified our hearts and souls during those days of joy and devotion. May we be blessed with happiness and joy, and may we be worthy to receive Thy blessings with gratitude and contentment. May all who worship Thy holy name be united by the spirit of harmony, love, and friendship. May the spirit of reverence and devotion, which our festivals have aroused, abide with us, that we may ever be ready to consecrate ourselves to Thy service.

"O Lord God, do Thou fill our hearts with feelings of sympathy and mercy, that we may be ever ready to extend a helping hand to those who are in distress, and bring relief to those that are in need of comfort and consolation. Grant peace and joy, blessings and comfort to all afflicted and destitute souls, and cause misery and suffering to vanish from the dwellers of the earth. AMEN."

At the morning services in the synagogue, Memorial Services (Yizkor) for the departed are read. Those unable to attend the synagogue services must read the Memorial Prayers at home. (For the Order of Memorial Services and the Yizkor Calendar, see pages 334-341).

SIMHAT TORAH   The ninth day of *Sukkot* is known as *Simhat Torah* (rejoicing of the Law). It is a day set aside especially for celebrating the granting of the Torah to the Jews. On this day, the reading of the Torah is concluded and commenced at the same time. It is customary with pious women to come to the synagogue on the eve of *Simhat Torah* and kiss the Scrolls as they are carried through the aisles. The procession is led by the *Hazzan* (cantor) who chants appropriate verses.

This day, too, must be observed as a strict festival, and only work allowable on all other festivals may be done. (See pages 142-143).

Upon lighting the festival candles on the eve of *Simhat Torah,* the two benedictions, recited on the first two days of *Sukkot,* are repeated. (See pages 179-180).

The following prayer is recited after lighting the festival candles on *Simhat Torah*:

"With great joy and gratitude, O Lord God, did I light the candles to celebrate this sublime Festival of joy, the sacred Feast when we conclude and begin anew Thy holy Torah. We delight to listen to the concluding words wherewith our holy Torah addresses itself to us, and with delight do we greet it again upon hearing the words wherewith our holy Torah begins.

"Father in heaven, we are very grateful unto Thee for Thy holy Torah which bestows upon us the richness of heavenly joy and gives us eternal life. The Torah is a tree of life whose fruit nourishes the spirit and rejoices the soul; it is the banner around which all the pious gather; it brings repose to the afflicted, and hope and faith to the drooping in spirit; it is the heavenly light that illumines the dark valley of the earth, and it brings cheer into the gloomy hut of misery and suffering.

"We therefore thank Thee, O heavenly Father, and praise Thy holy name for Thy having entrusted the people of Israel with such a precious jewel. We adore and worship Thee for Thy having enriched and elevated human life through Thy holy word, through Thy Law. Without the Torah, our life would be a barren, fearful dream, a ship without a guide upon the stormy sea.

"Almighty God, grant that Thy divine word may be ever alive within us, that it may ennoble and fortify our hearts, that it may strengthen our

faith in Thee in all sufferings and hardships, in
all joys and happiness that may come from Thee.
May the blessings of Thy Torah never depart
from our houses, from our children and the children of our children. May the brilliant rays of
Thy heavenly peace ever cheer us. AMEN."

THE HIGH HOLY DAYS

ROSH HASHANAH, NEW YEARS DAY
YOM KIPPUR, THE DAY OF ATONEMENT

*"Reflect upon three things, and thou wilt not fall
into sin: Know what is above thee, a seeing eye,
a hearing ear, and all thy deeds recorded in a book."*

(ABOT II, 1).

CHAPTER SIX

THE HIGH HOLY DAYS
ROSH HASHANAH AND YOM KIPPUR

1. ROSH HASHANAH [NEW YEARS DAY]

WHAT IS ROSH HASHANAH? Unlike all other major Jewish festivals, Rosh Hashanah is not connected with the festivities of the soil. It is purely a religious holiday, and marks the beginning of the Jewish year. It is observed on the first and second days of the Jewish month of Tishri, at the close of the summer season.

In the Bible, Rosh Hashanah is mentioned as the Day of Remembrance and as the Day of Blowing the Shofar (ram's horn). The Talmudic authorities know it by two additional names, Rosh Hashanah (New Year), and the Day of Judgment.

A SOLEMN FESTIVAL The Jew does not spend his New Years day in boisterous merrymaking and riotious festivity, but he welcomes this day with a spirit of awe and rev-

[193]

erence. He spends his Rosh Hashanah quietly, considering it as a day of reckoning with his God and his fellowman. He solemnly contemplates his moral and religious conduct of the past year, repenting, and resolving in his heart to let the teachings of the Almighty, as contained in His Torah, guide his acts during the incoming year.

A DAY OF JUDGMENT The Jew believes that New Years day is a day of judgment, whereon the Almighty sits as judge, so to say, and unfolds the records of every person's life, decreeing the destiny of each person for the year just begun. All destinies of mankind, individual and national, are recorded in heaven for the New Year in the Book of Life and in the Book of Death. At once the righteous are inscribed for life, the wicked are sentenced to death, and the indifferent are given ten days' time to repent.

On Rosh Hashanah, the Jew wholeheartedly prays for mercy and forgiveness. He pours out his bitter soul in prayer before his Father in heaven, convinced that the Almighty Judge, in His mercy and loving kindness, will answer his prayers and will inscribe the congregation of Israel in the Book of Life, Health and Happiness.

THE FESTIVAL CANDLES

On both evenings of Rosh Hashanah, the following two benedictions are pronounced when lighting the candles:

(On Sabbath add the words included in brackets).

בָּרוּךְ אַתָּה יְהוָֹה אֱלֹהֵינוּ, מֶלֶךְ הָעוֹלָם, אֲשֶׁר קִדְּשָׁנוּ בְּמִצְוֹתָיו, וְצִוָּנוּ לְהַדְלִיק נֵר שֶׁל (שַׁבָּת וְשֶׁל) יוֹם טוֹב.

"Barukh attah adonai elohenu melekh haolam, asher kidshanu bemitzvotav, vetzivanu lehadlik ner shel [shabbat veshel] yom tob."

"Praised art Thou, O Lord our God, King of the universe, who hast sanctified us by Thy commandments, and hast commanded us to kindle the [Sabbath and the] festival lights."

בָּרוּךְ אַתָּה יְהוָֹה אֱלֹהֵינוּ, מֶלֶךְ הָעוֹלָם, שֶׁהֶחֱיָנוּ וְקִיְּמָנוּ, וְהִגִּיעָנוּ לַזְּמַן הַזֶּה.

"Barukh attah adonai elohenu melekh haolam, sheheheyanu, vekiyemanu, vehigianu lazman hazzeh."

"Praised be Thou, O Lord our God, King of the universe, who hast granted us life, sustained us, and permitted us to reach this festive season."

On the second night of Rosh Hashanah, a

newly ripened fruit, which has not yet been tasted that season, is served for the second benediction over the candles.

After lighting the festival candles, the following prayer is recited:

"O Lord God, on this day of Rosh Hashanah, the first day of the New Year, I pray for Thy blessing. On this Day of Judgment, we more than ever realize that in Thy hand are our lives and our destinies. From Thee come life and death, riches and honor. Thou girdest the feeble with strength and endowest the despondent with new courage.

"Sovereign of the world! In thine infinite wisdom hast Thou decreed that on this solemn day we must call to mind the events of our past life. We have had our joys and ills, our sorrows, our successes, and our failures. But now, standing at the threshold of the New Year, I beseech Thee to strengthen our determination, for we wish to redeem the past. O help us develop whatever is good within us, so that we may turn unto Thee with a perfect repentance. Help us to learn to benefit from our shortcomings and our failures, so that we repeat not past errors.

Create in us a new heart and a new spirit, so that we strive to serve Thee in truth.

"Merciful Father! Extend Thy paternal care upon the widows and the orphans, the afflicted and the sorrowful. Pour Thine heavenly balm upon the wounded hearts, and be a protection to the forsaken and the persecuted. Send a perfect cure to the sick, and remove all sickness and sufferings from those who acknowledge Thy name. Comfort those that are burdened with sorrow, and proclaim a year of peace and good will to all ends of the earth, so that hatred and strife may forever cease.

"Great and holy God, bring to Thy people Israel new life, new strength and new hope, and grant them Thy protection. Grant hope to them that seek Thee, and confidence to them that wait for Thee. Bring back Israel's captivity, and have compassion upon them, and gather them again from amongst the peoples whither Thou hast scattered them.

"O Lord, let Thy heavenly light shine upon my children and upon the children of all Thy people Israel, that they may consecrate their lives to Thy service. Create in them a pure heart, O God, and a new spirit renew Thou

[197]

within them. Inscribe every member of my household and the households of all Israel in the Book of Life, Health, Sustenance and Peace.

"Hear our prayer, O Father; in Thee alone do we trust, for Thou art our shield and our redeemer. AMEN."

ROSH HASHANAH GREETINGS A comparatively new custom, that of exchanging New Year's greeting cards, is now widely observed. Cards are sent to relatives, friends, business associates, teachers, and so forth.

At the synagogue, after the evening service, the traditional Rosh Hashanah greeting, in Hebrew, is exchanged in a spirit of friendship, joy, and hope: *Leshanah tobah tikatebu* (may you be inscribed for a good year). Upon returning home from the synagogue from the Evening Service, the father greets his family with this traditional greeting.

A FESTIVAL OF REST The two days of Rosh Hashanah are to be strictly observed as a festival. All laws pertaining to other festivals must be observed: no manual labor is permitted except that which is necessary for the preparation of food for human beings. (See pages 142-143).

THE EVENING MEAL Although this festival is of a solemn nature, it must, like other holidays, be celebrated with joy and happiness. Rich meats and confectionary must be provided, and the meals should be even more elaborately served than on other festivals.

The evening meal is preceded by the Rosh Hashanah *kidush* (*Sanctification*), either over wine, or over two *hallot* (white loaves of bread), baked in the shape of a ladder or twist, symbolizing the hope that our prayers will go up to heaven. The ladder also reminds us that on Rosh Hashanah men are judged: some are destined to climb and prosper; others to descend and fail in their attempt.

At the evening meal, it is customary to symbolize the sweetness of the new year by dipping a slice of the *hallah* in honey after saying the *hamotzi* benediction. After eating this honey-dipped *hallah*—the amount to be eaten should be no less than the size of an olive— it is customary to say: "May it be Thy will, O Lord our God, to renew unto us a happy and pleasant year." A special effort is made by pious Jews to secure fish for the evening meal, because the fish symbolizes fruitfulness. The head of the family is served the head of the fish to symbolize our wish and hope that every one be "a head rather than a tail," that is, a leader among his fellows.

THE
SHOFAR
Everybody, man or woman, is obliged to hear the sound of the *shofar* (ram's horn) blown during the morning service at the synagogue, because the Almighty ordered that Rosh Hashanah shall be "a day of sounding the horn." If one of the two days of Rosh Hashanah falls on the Sabbath, the *shofar* is not sounded.

The plaintive notes of the ram's horn call to mind important historical events, sublime ideals, and hope and trust in God. The ram's horn commemorates the readiness with which Abraham prepared to sacrifice his only son Isaac before he was told to sacrifice a ram instead.

The blowing of the *shofar* calls Israel to rally to its God and exhorts it to a spirit of self analysis. The great Maimonides says that the notes of the *shofar* loudly call to the Jews: "Awake, ye that are sleepy, and ponder your deeds; remember your Creator, and go back to Him in penitence. Be not of those who miss reality in their hunt after shadows, and waste their years in seeking after vain things which can neither profit nor deliver. Look well to your souls and consider your deeds; let each one of you forsake his evil ways and thoughts, and return to God, so that He may have mercy on you."

The *shofar* also recalls how the children of Israel received the Ten Commandments at Mount Sinai to the accompaniment of *shofar* blasts. The Jew is further reminded by the plaintive notes of the *shofar* of the tragic destruction of the Temple in Jerusalem, and of the centuries of suffering that followed. But it also recalls to the Jewish heart the promise of redemption, when the prophet Elijah will appear to announce the arrival of the Messiah, and from the top of the mountains will sound the mighty *shofar* of freedom and of equality of mankind.

THE FAST OF GEDALIAH Immediately following the second day of Rosh Hashanah, the third of Tishri, the Jews observe the fast of Gedaliah. (See page 258 why this fast day is observed).

THE TEN DAYS OF REPENTANCE The first day of Rosh Hashanah ushers in a period of penitence which ends with Yom Kippur, the Day of Atonement. These ten days are known as *aseret yeme teshubah* (the

[201]

Ten Days of Penitence), and are observed with awe and solemnity both in the synagogue and in the home.

According to the Jewish belief, the wicked and the indifferent are given ten days' time within which to repent. On Rosh Hashanah the destiny of all mankind is recorded and written down, while on Yom Kippur the seal is attached to the decree. If the wicked repent before Yom Kippur, the decree is changed, and they are granted a good and happy New Year.

2. YOM KIPPUR

THE DAY OF ATONEMENT

WHAT IS YOM KIPPUR? This very solemn day, Yom Kippur (Day of Atonement), is observed on the tenth day of the month of Tishri. As decreed by God in His Law, the Jews must afflict themselves on this day, because their sins will be forgiven by Him. On this day the destiny of all mankind is sealed by the Heavenly Court. Repentance, Prayer and Charity will avert an evil decree. Therefore the whole day of Yom Kippur is spent at the synagogue, repenting, praying, and donating to charitable institutions.

Yom Kippur is a day of self-retrospection. Every Jew must solemnly contemplate his past conduct, repent, and resolve to improve and follow the ways of his God in the future.

THE FINAL DECREE On Yom Kippur the decree of all mankind, as written down on Rosh Hashanah, is sealed. On this day, the deeds of man are considered and weighed. If the good deeds outweigh the bad, the man is declared deserving. If the bad deeds outweigh the good, the man is considered undeserving. Sins, however, are forgiven as a result of sincere repentance, prayers and charity.

WHAT SINS ARE FORGIVEN Repentance, prayer and charity on the Day of Atonement obtain mercy and forgiveness from the Almighty for sins committed against Him, but they do not atone for the transgressions committed against a fellowman. Such sins will be forgiven you by the Almighty only when you conciliate the person you have wronged. If, therefore, you have a money dispute with your fellowman notify him, on the day before Yom Kippur, that immediately after Yom Kippur you will submit the case before the proper tribunal for decision, and that you will honestly and sincerely abide by the decision of that tribunal. Even if you have sinned against your fellowman by slander or by tale-bearing, it is your duty to go to him and ask his forgiveness. Otherwise the Almighty will not forgive your sins, no matter how fervently you pray, or how solemnly you repent of your actions.

If any one seeks your forgiveness for having wronged you, do not cruelly refuse him, but grant him forgiveness willingly and whole-

heartedly. A Jew must follow the ways and attributes of the Lord our God, by being slow of
anger and easily appeased. Even if you have
been grievously wronged, you should not seek
vengeance, nor bear a grudge against the one
that wronged you. It is the way of the truly
pious to forgive all those who have wronged
them during the year, whether such persons
ask their forgiveness or not. If you harbor
enmity in your heart, your prayers will not be
heard in heaven on Yom Kippur; but if you
are magnanimous and forgiving, all your sins
will be forgiven by the Almighty.

MIDDAY MEAL The day before Yom Kippur is considered a holiday among Jews. It is a
mitzvah (religious duty) to prepare
a sumptuous feast and to fare generously on
this day. In fact, our sages say that it is so
virtuous to feast well on the day before Yom
Kippur that it is equivalent to fasting on Yom
Kippur itself. It is a *mitzvah* to eat fish at
this meal.

KAPPAROT During the existence of the Temple
at Jerusalem, the Jews sacrificed animals as a substitute for their own lives. On every
Yom Kippur, a scape-goat (*azazel*) was sent

from the Temple into the desert, to carry away
the sins of the people. With the destruction of
the second Temple by the Romans, the sacrificing of animals ceased, and as a means of offering a ransom, the custom of *kapparot* was introduced. They chose for their ransom (*kapparot*) a chicken, or any other fowl, upon the
head of which each man laid his sins. Men
generally select roosters and women hens; they
swing the fowl above their heads three times,
reciting: "This fowl is my substitute and my
ransom, and shall be killed that I may survive
for a long and peaceful life." Some people
prefer white fowl, because white symbolizes
purity and innocence. The fowl is killed and
cooked, and served at the fast meal on the eve
of Yom Kippur. Persons unable to procure
a live fowl substitute for it a few coins which
they swing above their heads and recite: "This
coin is my substitute and my ransom, and shall
be given for charity that I may survive for a
long and peaceful life." The *kapparot* ceremony is performed either in the morning or
on the night before Yom Kippur.

Many famous Rabbis, among them the
great Maimonides, were strongly opposed to the
custom of *kapparot*, yet it still survives.

THE FAST-MEAL An hour before sunset on the day before Yom Kippur, Jews partake of the fast-meal, which marks the end of all eating and drinking until after the appearance of the stars the following evening. The *hallot* baked for this occasion are formed in the shape of ladders. (What this shape symbolizes, see page 199). Either at this meal or at the middy meal, some people are accustomed to serve soup containing *kreplach*, small pieces of noodle-dough folded in triangular form and stuffed with ground meat. As on New Year, it is customary to dip a piece of the *hallah* in honey. Food which is easy to digest should be served at this meal. It is customary not to serve fish on this occasion. Eating spicy food should be avoided, as neither water nor food may be had after concluding the Grace at the end of the meal. If you finish your meal long before sunset, and you intend to eat or drink after the final meal, you must either expressly say so or bear it in mind before saying the Grace after the meal.

BLESSING THE CHILDREN It is customary with some fathers and mothers to bless their children before going to the synagogue on Yom Kippur eve, because the holiness of the day has already become effective and the gates of mercy are already open to our prayers. In this blessing, the parents pray that their children may be granted a happy life, and that their hearts may be firm in the fear of God.

The following is an appropriate prayer for the occasion.

"May the Lord render you like Ephraim and Manasseh. (For daughters: May the Lord render you like Sarah, Rebecca, Rachel and Leah).

"Merciful Father, aid my children to see and understand that sin is folly and virtue is wisdom, and that 'the beginning of wisdom is the fear of the Lord.' Create in them a pure heart, and renew a right spirit within them.

"Almighty God, help my children to see that sin is weakness, and the yielding to temptation as lack of power of will. Bestow upon them a new strength, a heavenly spiritual strength, so that they can overcome and destroy the enemy, the evil inclination, within their heart.

"O God, grant them understanding to know and perceive that the selfish, the idle and the shirker do not live. The soul that sins dies. He alone lives who lives worthily and abides

by Thy holy commandments; for he who findeth
Thee findeth life. May they always choose the
path of life.

"O inscribe us all in Thy book of life,
health and happiness. AMEN."

LIGHTING
THE
CANDLES

It is our duty to honor this holy
day of Yom Kippur by wearing
clean apparel and by lighting many
lights at home as well as at the synagogue. At the synagogue, the scrolls of the
Torah are draped in white mantles, and the
Ark in which the scrolls are contained is adorned
with white curtains; the tables are decked with
white covers, and many lights are lit.

As on Sabbath-eve, about a half hour before sundown, the candles are lit, and the benediction is recited:

(On the Sabbath add the words included
in the brackets).

בָּרוּךְ אַתָּה יְהֹוָה אֱלֹהֵינוּ, מֶלֶךְ הָעוֹלָם, אֲשֶׁר קִדְּשָׁנוּ בְּמִצְוֹתָיו,
וְצִוָּנוּ לְהַדְלִיק נֵר שֶׁל (שַׁבָּת וְשֶׁל) יוֹם הַכִּפּוּרִים.

"Barukh attah adonai elohenu melekh
haolam, asher kidshanu bemitzvotav, vetzivanu
lehadlik ner shel [shabbat veshel] yom hakki-
purim."

"Praised be Thou, O Lord our God, King of
the universe, who hast sanctified us by Thy

commandments, and hast commanded us to kindle the lights of the [Sabbath and of the] Day of Atonement."

Then the following prayer is recited:

"Almighty God, who art merciful and gracious, long-suffering and abundant in kindness, look down with pity upon us. I have sinned before Thee, and now I ask and desire of Thee mercy and forgiveness, on the Day of Atonement, set apart by Thee for the purification of our hearts and the renewal of our spiritual life.

"I humbly thank Thee, O Lord, for Thy having entrusted unto me the privilege of fulfilling the precept of kindling the lights on this holy day of Yom Kippur, and pray that Thou favorably accept my supplication. Our sins and transgressions are many, and we need Thy pardoning grace. For shouldst Thou mark all our failings, O Lord, who would be able to stand before Thee?

"O Father, to Thee our innermost life is revealed, and Thou knowest all our thoughts, even those which remain buried in our bosom. O deal kindly with us, as we humble ourselves before Thee and seek Thy mercy and forgiveness. We confess our transgressions and shortcomings before Thee, and we implore of Thee not to forsake us, and to grant us forgiveness and peace.

"O Lord, help us to banish all hatred and vindictiveness from our hearts, and help us to strive to be at peace with our fellowmen. If we are guilty of having done them any wrong or injustice, may this day of Yom Kippur admonish us, that we dare not ask Thy pardon before we have done our utmost to pacify those against whom we have offended, until we have undone the evil we have caused. We are ready to forgive and pardon all those who have wronged us, and may they, too, be ready and willing to forgive us for all wrong done to them. O give us the courage to acknowledge our sins to our fellowmen, and thus restore the bonds of friendship and heal the wounds we have inflicted. Reconciled to one another as brothers and sisters, we may call unto Thee as our Father to accept our supplications and to send unto us that light and comfort which we crave according to our trials and necessities.

"O may this Holy Day come as a messenger of peace and consolation to all our brethren of the house of Israel throughout their habitations. May Jersualem and the Holy Temple be rebuilt speedily in our days. Hear us, O God, and answer us according to the fullness of Thy mercy. AMEN."

A DAY OF AFFLICTION Because the Almighty said that Yom Kippur shall be a day of affliction to us, our sages decreed that on this day, even when it occurs on the Sabbath, we must abstain from: eating, drinking, bathing, anointing (massaging), wearing shoes, and cohabitation.

Only bathing and washing for pleasure is forbidden, but if one is ill, one may wash oneself on Yom Kippur. A bride within thirty days of her wedding may wash her face on Yom Kippur, so that she may not become repulsive to her husband.

Anointing or massaging even a part of the body is forbidden on Yom Kippur. However if one is ill, even though not dangerously ill, one is permited to anoint or massage oneself.

Only leather shoes are forbidden on Yom Kippur, but shoes of other material may be worn. One who is even slightly indisposed, however, or one who has a bruised foot, or a woman within thirty days of her confinement may wear leather shoes on Yom Kippur.

Women in confinement, or persons dangerously sick should at their request be given food on Yom Kippur, lest fasting impair or endanger their health. Even if many physicians agree that fasting will not harm them but on the contrary will help them, nevertheless, their request for food must be complied with, because in eating and drinking the judgment of the sick is held more reliable: the sufferer is the best judge of his condition.

If the appetite of a pregnant woman is awakened by the aroma of food, and if she shows it either by word or by the expression of her face, she is quietly told that it is the Day of Atonement. This information often has the effect of allaying her desire. If, in spite of this, she still wants the food, she is first given a taste of it, on the theory that one drop or one crumb will often tend to quench her appetite. She must, however, be given as much as she desires.

A child less than nine years old should not be permitted to fast even part of the day, because it may undermine his health. A child fully nine years old and in good health should be trained to fast gradually. He may at first be made to abstain from food for a few hours beyond his regular eating time.

A DAY OF REST Yom Kippur is a holy day to the Lord our God, and on that day everybody, man or woman, must abstain from doing any sort of manual labor and from transacting any business. In this respect, all laws

effective on the Sabbath must be observed on
Yom Kippur.

KOL NIDRE EVE Seeking forgiveness of one's wronged neighbors is done before the beginning of the service of Kol Nidre, which starts before sunset.

Before the *Kol Nidre* service, pious men generally put on white robes (*kittels*), which stand for purity and innocence. The *kittel* serves as a reminder of humility to soften arrogant hearts, because white robes are also used for burial. On the *kittel* they put the *tallit* (the fringed garment). The women, too, are as a rule dressed in white.

It is a holy evening. With solemn faces, all await the opening of the service. Now the curtains from the Ark are drawn, the congregation rises, the Scrolls are taken out, and the *hazzan* (cantor) sings that inspiring melody, *kol nidre*. Thrice he chants it, while the congregation listens attentively.

YOM KIPPUR DAY Pious Jews spend the whole day of Yom Kippur at the synagogue, fasting, praying, and liberally responding to appeals made for various charitable institutions. Women are not exempt from these duties. With contrite spirit and broken heart, they read the prayer *al het* (Confession), which contains a long list of sins, such as cruelty, dishonesty, disrespect for parents and elders, slander, arrogance, and treachery; and they ask the Almighty for forgiveness.

MEMORIAL SERVICE On the Day of Atonement, Memorial prayers arc said for the departed, because remembrance of the dead breaks a man's pride and humbles his heart. Another reason for Memorial Prayers on Yom Kippur is that the dead, too, need atonement, and therefore offerings of charity are made for their souls. By giving charity and praying, the living are able to lighten the judgment of the dead in the world to come, and in return the pious souls of the departed plead for the living ones who remember them. (For the order of Memorial Services and the Yizkor Calendar, see pages 334-341).

THE CONCLUSION OF THE DAY The final prayer of the day is the *neilah* (closing) prayer. It is so called, because during the whole day of Yom Kippur, the gates of heaven are open to receive and accept prayers and supplications. While the sun is reddening the tops of the trees, the gates of mercy slowly close. At the time of the closing of the gates, we beg for special mercy and favor, and with more fervor than ever supplicate the Almighty. At the end of the service the *shofar* (ram's horn) is sounded once, and with this the Holy Day is brought to a close.

The *hazzan* (cantor) recites the *habdalah* over wine, and upon coming home, every pious Jew repeats the *habdalah* over wine. (For the definition of *habdalah*, see page 134).

AT HOME Before leaving the synagogue, greetings are exchanged with the traditional words *gemar hatimah tobah* (a favorable final sealing, or verdict). Coming home, there should be eating, drinking, and rejoicing, thereby indicating that the Jews are confident that they have obtained mercy from heaven. The Jews are encouraged again by the words of our sages who said: "On the conclusion of the Day of Atonement, a heavenly voice goes forth saying: 'Go, eat thy bread with joy, and drink thy wine with a merry heart, for God has already accepted thy deeds favorably.' "

CHAPTER SEVEN
THE MINOR FESTIVALS

HANUKKAH, THE FESTIVAL OF LIGHTS
PURIM, WHEN THE JEW LAUGHS
LAG BAOMER,
THE SCHOOL CHILDREN'S FESTIVAL
ROSH HODESH, NEW MOON
HAMISHAH ASAR BISHEVAT,
THE JEWISH ARBOR DAY

כוס
אליהו
הנבי

NOTA KOSLOWSKY

THE MINOR FESTIVALS

1. HANUKKAH

THE FESTIVAL OF LIGHTS

WHAT IS HANUKKAH? In Hebrew, *Hanukkah* means dedication. It is the name of a festival that recalls the triumph of the Jews over the Syrians and Greeks. These heathen nations had forcibly taken possession of God's Temple in Jerusalem and dedicated it to their idol-god Zeus. The Jewish people, whose numbers were small in comparison with the mighty Grecian armies, fought many stubborn and brave battles against their enemies, and drove them out of Jerusalem, once more dedicating the Holy Temple to the God of Israel. They then celebrated the festival of dedication for eight days by illuminating the Temple and their homes.

All this happened over two thousand years ago, but the Jews in every land, year after year still celebrate the festival of Hanukkah with great merriment and joy. For eight days, beginning with the twenty-fifth day of the month of Kislev, the Jews in every home light the Hanukkah lamp with its eight small candles.

The children and the grown-ups as well indulge in all sorts of games, and offer special prayers of thanksgiving to the Almighty.

These tiny candles, despite their feeble light, recall a wonderful story of God's salvation of the Jews from ruin and destruction. They bring to mind the story of the world's first heroes, under the leadership of the unforgetable Maccabean family, who fought and died for the freedom of worship and religion. They teach that those who have faith in God never fail, and that right prevails over might.

And this is why it is written: "Judah Maccabee, his brothers, and the whole congregation of Israel ordained that the days of the Dedication of the Temple, Hanukkah, should be celebrated from year to year for eight days, beginning with twenty-fifth day of Kislev, with praise and thanksgiving to the Almighty."

THE MEANING OF HANUKKAH TODAY

Recently Hanukkah has become a very important festival. The Festival of Lights brings, not only to Jews but to all people, a message of idealism, courage and hope. Today, more than ever, the Jew is in need of the old Maccabean spirit to contend with his enemies abroad and in his midst.

In spite of the frightful persecution and hatred which the Jew has suffered through the ages, he still lives on, adhering to his teachings and ideals. The miracle of the Jewish people is told by the tiny candles that are lit on Hanukkah. Their weak glow tell the story of the eternal people.

The pioneers, Haluzzim, settling in Palestine to rebuild the Jewish homeland, are urged on by Maccabean courage and hope. In spite of all obstacles, they keep on building and building; ceaselessly and tirelessly they improve and cultivate the Palestinian soil. They do it not for themselves, but for their people and for the future generations. These pioneers are indeed imbued with the spirit of God, and inspired by superhuman courage and boldness. Who can fathom or understand the Jewish soul?

THE HANUKKAH SPIRIT In his feasting and celebrating, the Jew is never selfish. He does not keep the joy for himself alone, but shares it with others less fortunate than himself. During the eight days of Hanukkah, when he is happy, forgetting for a while his dangerous enemies in celebrating and feasting, he liberally donates charity to the poor and needy in his community.

As the main object of the Grecian oppressors was to undermine and destroy the Jewish religion and the Law of God, there has developed the beautiful custom among Jews to give liberal gifts for the special purpose of supporting and maintaining poor students engaged in the study of the Law. And for the same reason it has become the custom for pupils to make gifts to their Hebrew teachers during the Hanukkah festival. These gifts are known as *Hanukkah-Gelt* (Hanukkah Money).

But those are not the only ones to receive *Hanukkah-Gelt*. On Hanukkah, the children receive *Hanukkah-Gelt* from their fathers, and Hanukkah gifts from their mothers, brothers, sisters, and friends.

HANUKKAH CELEBRATION Unlike all other Jewish festivals, Hanukkah is marked by no special feasting. No elaborate meal is prescribed by law or custom for the occasion. The only special dish introduced by custom of long standing is Hanukkah *latkes,* potatoe or other kind of pan-cakes, which are eaten during the eight days of Hanukkah.

In some localities, it is also customary to prepare dairy meals in which cheese predominates. This is to commemorate the story of a brave Jewish woman Judith, who risked her life to save a Jewish community. (1)

HANUKKAH
LAMP

Hanukkah is the festival of lights, to indicate that light—the symbol of wisdom, understanding, right and justice—prevails over darkness, ignorance, injustice and intolerance.

In every synagogue and in every Jewish home, the Hanukkah lamp is prepared for the lighting of candles on the eve of the twenty-fifth day of the month of Kislev. The lamp is of metal—usually, of copper—and is, as a rule, decorated with such symbols as, lions, eagles, vines and pomegranates. It has eight branches for the eight candles to be lit during Hanukkah, and one special branch to hold the *shamesh*. The *shamesh*, or the servile candle, is lit first by the one officiating, and is used to light the other candles over which he pronounces the benedictions. Some Hanukkah lamps are oil-burning and are provided with wicks instead of candles.

(1) See, Goldin, Book of Legends, Part III, Chapter V).

WHO MUST LIGHT THE HANUKKAH LAMP? Every man and every woman must observe the commandment of lighting the Hanukkah lamp, because everybody, man as well as woman, was benefited by the miracles of Hanukkah. Even children, provided they are old enough to be trained and tutored, must be taught to light the Hanukkah lamp.

In some communities, it is customary for every member of the household to light the Hanukkah lamp, and pronounce the benedictions over it. In others, the head of the family alone lights the lamp, pronouncing the benedictions, while all the members of the household gather around and listen attentively, saying *Amen* at the end of each benediction.

WHEN THE LAMP MUST BE LIT Late in the afternoon of the twenty-fourth day of Kislev, immediately after nightfall and the appearance of the stars the Hanukkah lamp is lit. The time for the lighting of the Hanukkah lamp must not be deliberately delayed.

During the eight days of Hanukkah all kinds of work may be done, although it is customary to do no work after the Hanukkah lamp has been lit.

On Sabbath eve, the Hanukkah lamp must be lit before the Sabbath candles.

At the close of the Sabbath, the *Habdalah* ceremony must be performed before the Hanukkah lamp is lit.

SIZE OF CANDLES Candles for the Hanukkah lamp must be large enough to burn at least half an hour. During this half hour, it is forbidden for any one to make use of the light shed by the Hanukkah candles, either for reading, or working, or the like. The lights are to serve solely to celebrate Hanukkah.

On Sabbath eve, when the Hanukkah candles must be lit earlier than on week-days, it is necessary that the Hanukkah candles be large enough to keep burning for no less than thirty minutes after the appearance of the stars, as otherwise the benedictions pronounced over them are of no value.

HOW THE CANDLES ARE LIT On the first evening of Hanukkah, one candle is lit over which the benedictions are pronounced; on the second night, two candles; on the third, three; and thus one more is added each evening until the eighth when all the eight candles are lit. The order of arranging and lighting the candles is as follows: On the first evening the candle to be lit is placed at the right end of the Hanukkah lamp. On the second evening one is added towards the left; and on every succeeding evening one candle is added always towards the left. The newly-added candle must be lit first, immediately after the benedictions are pronounced, and then the lighting of the rest of the candles is continued towards the right.

On the first evening of Hanukkah, whoever lights the Hanukkah lamp recites three benedictions before lighting. On the other evenings, only the first two of those three are pronounced.

ORDER OF LIGHTING THE HANUKKAH LAMP The three benedictions to be recited on lighting the *Hanukkah* lamp:

בָּרוּךְ אַתָּה יְהֹוָה אֱלֹהֵינוּ, מֶלֶךְ הָעוֹלָם, אֲשֶׁר קִדְּשָׁנוּ בְּמִצְוֹתָיו, וְצִוָּנוּ לְהַדְלִיק נֵר שֶׁל חֲנֻכָּה.

"Barukh attah adonai, elohenu melekh haolam, asher kidshanu bemitzvotav, vetzivanu lehadlik ner shel hanukkah."

"Praised be Thou, O Lord our God, King of the universe, who hast sanctified us by Thy

comandments, and hast bidden us to kindle the
Hanukkah lights."

בָּרוּךְ אַתָּה יְהוָֹה אֱלֹהֵינוּ, מֶלֶךְ הָעוֹלָם, שֶׁעָשָׂה נִסִּים לַאֲבוֹתֵינוּ
בַּיָּמִים הָהֵם בַּזְּמַן הַזֶּה.

"Barukh attah adonai, elohenu melekh
haolam, sheasah nissim laabotenu bayamim
hahem, bazman hazzeh."

"Praised be Thou, O Lord our God, King
of the universe, who didst wondrous things for
our fathers at this season in those days."

(The following benediction is recited on
the first night only).

בָּרוּךְ אַתָּה יְהוָֹה אֱלֹהֵינוּ, מֶלֶךְ הָעוֹלָם, שֶׁהֶחֱיָנוּ וְקִיְּמָנוּ, יְהִגִּיעָנוּ
לַזְּמַן הַזֶּה.

"Barukh attah adonai, elohenu melekh
haolam, sheheheyanu, vekiyemanu, vehigianu
lazman hazzeh."

"Praised be Thou, O Lord our God, King
of the universe, who hast granted us life, sustained us, and permitted us to reach this festive
season."

(After kindling the Hanukkah lamp, the
following prayer is recited).

"We kindle these lights on account of the
miracles, the deliverance and the wonders which
Thou didst for our fathers, through Thy holy

priests. During all the eight days of Hanukkah these lights are sacred, and we are not permitted to make profane use of them, but we are just to look at them, in order that we may give thanks to Thy name for Thy miracles, Thy deliverance and Thy wonders."

(An appropriate prayer for the first night of Hanukkah).

"Our God and God of our fathers, with grateful hearts we remember today Thy protection of old, when tyrants sought to destroy Thy people Israel and to uproot its religion. We recall with joyful pride the Maccabean courage and valor. We think with reverence of the faith of the Jewish heroes in Thy name and of their devotion to Thy Law, when the wicked king Antiochus designed to undermine Thy Law and enforce idol-worship among Israel. We commemorate the rededication of Thy sanctuary and the consecration of its altar unto Thy worship, when the tyrants in their presumptuousness dared to place a despicable idol on Thine altar in the holy Temple at Jerusalem. We celebrate the rekindling of the perpetual lamp, whose rays shone forth out of the encircling darkness, as the symbol of Thy presence and the beacon light of Thy truth and love for all mankind. And we pour forth our thankful praises for the tender care and unfailing love with which Thou didst guard our fathers in those days and at all times.

"O Lord God, be with us and our children today. Imbue us with perfect faith in Thee. Make us strong to do Thy will. Bless the Hanukkah lights that they may shed their radiance into our homes and our lives. May they kindle within us the flame of faith and zeal so that, like the Maccabees of old, we may battle bravely for Thy cause. Make us worthy of Thy love and Thy blessing, our Shield and Protector. Let injustice and oppression cease, and cruelty, hatred, and wrong pass away, so that all men may unite to worship Thy holy name.

"O merciful Father, send us Thy deliverer speedily in our days, and may we behold the redemption of Thy people Israel, when Thou wilt return to Zion, Thy Holy City, and end the bitter exile of the children of Abraham, Isaac and Jacob. AMEN."

HANUKKAH GAMES The Jew generally looks with disfavor upon the playing of games. On Hanukkah, however, he allows the playing of games, provided they are not played for money. During Hanukkah, after the evening meal, people usually indulge in playing such games as checkers, chess, dominoes, and cards.

The younger children play with the Hanukkah *draidel*, a revolving die, on the four sides of which are marked the Hebrew letters: נ (nun); ג (gimmel); ה (he); and שׁ (shin). These four letters stand for the four words:

שָׁם	הָיָה	גָּדוֹל	נֵס
There	was	a great	miracle

These four letters also indicate the result of each game. If after the die is spun by one of the players the letter נ (nun) comes out on the top, the spinner gets nothing, because the *nun* stands for the Jewish word "nichts," *nothing.* If the letter ג (gimmel) comes out on the top, the player takes all, because *gimmel* stands for "gantz," *all;* if it is a ה (he), the player gets half, because the *he* stands for "halb," *half;* if it is the letter שׁ (shin), the player must add to the stakes, because this letter stands for "stell," *put* or *add.*

HANUKKAH
IN
AMERICA
In former years, Hanukkah was primarily a home festival. But to-day, especially in America, it is gradually becoming a community festival.

The spirit of Hanukkah is felt in Jewish

and Hebrew schools and clubs. Almost every Hebrew school has a Hanukkah play in which many young pupils participate. Many schools have special assemblies, public entertainments and class-room parties. Youth clubs generally present Hanukkah plays, and make collections for the Jewish National Fund to buy land in Palestine.

2. PURIM

ON PURIM THE JEW LAUGHS

Purim is the Jew's day of laughter. It is his day of dancing, merry-making, feasting and drinking. No matter that the Jew has always discouraged the use of intoxicating liquor. On Purim, the sages say, a Jew must drink until he is so thoroughly muddled that he no longer knows whether to curse Haman or bless Mordecai.

On Purim the Jew displays the greatness of his soul, his unswerving faith in his God and his people. Haman, the hater of the Jews, and the Jew Mordecai, who obstinately insists on worshiping God in his own way, are not mere figures in history. Hamans are to be found in every land where there are Mordecais, Jews determined to observe their traditions of life and thought.

The Jew laughs; he does not lose courage. He mocks the Hamans who seek to destroy him. He knows that right and not might will eventually triumph. He is convinced that in the end the obstinate Mordecais will overcome the heartless Hamans who will meet their down-fall, as did Haman of old. Therefore, the Jew celebrates Purim with all his heart.

WHAT IS PURIM? The holiday takes its name from the Hebrew word *purim,* meaning *lots.* Long ago, when the Persians gained dominion over the land of Judah, a whimsical, foolish king, Ahasuerus, swayed by his wicked prime-minister Haman agreed to destroy all the Jews in his domain. Having been warned that all enemies of the Jews have met with failure, Haman, being superstitious, decided to cast lots and determine the most favorable day for the slaughter. The lots indicated that day to be the thirteenth day of the twelfth month, Adar.

Haman, of course, could not have foreseen that these lots would furnish a name for his intended victims' most joyous festival. He could not have known that his plot had been doomed to failure by the Almighty who had prepared the remedy for the blow long before the blow could be struck.

It happened that before Haman was appointed prime-minister, King Ahasuerus had executed his first queen, Vashti, for disobedience, and had then chosen in her place the charming

Jewish maiden Esther. When the king, yielding to Haman's wish, decreed death for all the Jews, Mordecai, Queen Esther's cousin, induced her to intercede for her people. By her plea to the king the Jews were saved.

Therefore the Jews then ordained that, "They and their children should keep two days of Purim every year, throughout every generation, every family in every province and in every town; that the days of Purim never be blotted out from the memory of the Jews." Ever since then Jews all over the world have celebrated Purim each year on the fourteenth and fifteenth days of Adar with feasting and gladness.

IMPORTANCE
OF PURIM
may be performed on Purim. Purim is not a holiday in the strict sense of the word. Manual labor Even in localities where it is customary not to work on Purim, the transaction of business is permitted, and one may write whatever letters one pleases.

Although in these respects Purim is a minor holiday, the Jews consider it nevertheless, one of very great importance. The Talmudic sages say that Purim would be observed by the Jews forever, even when all other holidays would be forgotten.

ESTHER'S FAST The day before Purim — the thirteenth day of Adar—is a day of fasting for the Jew. He neither eats nor drinks until after the evening reading of the Scroll of Esther. This day is known as the "Fast of Esther," because Queen Esther, before going to King Ahasuerus to plead for her people begged Mordecai to have all the Jews of Shushan fast for three days. Therefore all the Jews, in the days of Mordecai and Esther, established one of these three days, the thirteenth of Adar, as a public fast day for all generations to come. To this day, the Jew, faithful to the ordinances of his sages, fasts on this day, and prays to be rid of the modern Hamans.

If Purim falls on a Sunday, the Fast of Esther is observed on the preceding Thursday, the eleventh of Adar, because on Saturday no fasting is allowed, except when Yom Kippur occurs thereon, and to fast on Friday would interfere with the preparations for the Sabbath. If, however, one mistakenly neglected to fast on Thursday, one must then do so on Friday, the twelfth of Adar.

PREPARATION FOR PURIM During the fast of Esther, Jewish housewives busy themselves with preparing the Purim feast. A special kind of baking has beeen adopted for this occasion. Some of the dishes have names symbolic of the historical events to be commemorated. There will be the three-cornered breads or cakes, filled with poppy-seeds or with chopped prunes and raisins. These have become known as *Hamantaschen,* after the triangular cap which Haman is believed to have worn. In some localities it is the custom to bake *kreplach* for Purim. This is a three-cornered fritter, filled with minced meat, and boiled either in soup or separately and served with soup.

READING THE MEGILLAH *Megillah,* scroll, is the name given to one of the biblical works, the Book of Esther, in which the story of Purim is told. Many years ago, the Great Sanhedrin, of which Mordecai is said to have been a member, ordained that the *megillah* be read on Purim, both on the evening of the thirteenth day of the month of Adar, and again on the morning of the following day. Everyone, man, woman and child, is obliged to hear the *megillah* read. And because the reading of the *megillah* is considered a festive event, the Jew must put on his best clothes when going to the synagogue for the occasion. Upon his return home, he must find the lights lit and the table set in token of the evening's festivities.

Those unable to go to the synagogue must hear the *megillah* read at home. Whenever possible, however, it should be read among a multitude of people, or at least in the presence of a *minion*, a quorum of ten male adults.

Towards evening, the Jews assemble in their synagogues to hear the story of Haman's downfall and Mordecai's victory. They bring along their children that they may be trained from early youth to hear the *megillah* read.

After the stars become visible to the naked eye, but not before, the reader unrolls the whole *megillah*, and recites three benedictions, each of which is answered by all present with a hearty *Amen*. Then slowly, in a measured tone and in the traditional melody, the reader chants the contents of the *megillah*. Everyone listens attentively to each and every word, for should one miss a single word, one's obligation to hear the *megillah* read has not been fulfilled.

The Jew reveres the synagogue where he worships his God, and he permits nothing to be done or said there which might imply contempt for the holy place. But on Purim, when he makes sport of the Hamans of the past and of the present, the Jew allows and sometimes even encourages conduct which on other days would be impermissible in the synagogue.

Coming to the synagogue, the children are given toy pistols and rattles of all kinds, commonly known as *gragers*. At the mention of the name of Haman, the children begin shaking their rattles and shooting their guns, while the adults hiss, stamp and shout, until the place is alive with noise.

MERRYMAKING ON PURIM The Jew, as a rule, celebrates his festivals with merriment, but at the same time with a certain degree of reserve and solemnity in accordance with his religious principles and traditions. Frivolity or intoxication he does not tolerate.

Purim, however, is a special occasion. *Purim spielers,* Purim-players, men and youngsters dressed in funny clothes, go about the streets singing Purim-songs, dancing, joking, and performing clowning tricks for which they receive a few coins. Some stage Purim-plays consisting of certain topics having a direct bearing upon the Purim festival.

On this day of merrymaking, boys and girls walk from house to house in grotesque masks and indulge in all kinds of jollity. They are often given a few coins for singing comic songs, one of the most popular of which is: "Heint is Purim, morgen is aus, git mir a penny, und warft mir heraus." (Today is Purim, tomorrow it is over; give me a cent, and you can throw me out).

CHARITY ON PURIM—SHALAH-MANOT On Purim, the Jew not only displays his faith in God, but also the generosity of his heart. Mordecai commanded the Jews to "make the Purim-days as days of feasting and gladness, and of sending portions to one another, and gifts to the poor."

Faith and charity are therefore essentials in the celebration of Purim. On every festival the poor are remembered and surely they are not to be neglected on Purim. Toward evening, before Purim has set in and before the reading of the *megillah*, the Jew begins to provide for taking care of his poor. It is customary for every Jew to give half the unit coin current in the country, to commemorate the half-shekel the Jews were accustomed to give for the buying of the public sacrifices during the existence of the Temple in Jerusalem. These contributions are known as *mahazit hashekel*, half a shekel. The general practice is for every person to give three half-shekels; but some give half-shekels according to the number of persons in the family. The money is then distributed among the poor.

On Purim even the poorest Jew who is himself dependent upon charitable contributions, is obliged to give at least two gifts to two persons, one gift to each. Whoever is willing to accept charity must be allowed to participate. If one lives in a community where there are no people willing to accept charity, one must either send the Purim-money to charitable institutions, or keep it until one meets poor persons who will accept it. Women, too, must contribute charity on this day.

On Purim the Jew also complies with the law of *sending portions to one another.* Everybody, man and woman alike, must send at least two gifts to one of their friends, no matter whether this friend is rich or poor. Strictly speaking, these gifts must be of food which may be eaten without further preparation, such as boiled meats, confectionery, fruits and wines. One may not give raw foods or other articles. But the custom now prevails to include in the *shalah-manot* gifts such items as books, wearing apparel, and other useful articles.

Although it is well to have great feasts on Purim and to send many gifts to friends

and neighbors, yet it is held far more praiseworthy to give to the poor. It is said that
there is no more greater joy and no more glorious deed before the Holy One than the glad-
dening of the hearts of those in need.

THE
PURIM
SEUDAH

Purim must be celebrated by feasting;
and so every Jewish family must enjoy at least one festival meal, to be
begun toward the evening of the
fourteenth of Adar. This meal is known as
seudat Purim, Purim feast.

The *Purim seudah* is a happy family din-
ner. Food and drink are of the best. The
Hamantaschen (the triangular shaped breads),
and the *kreplach* (three-cornered fritters), prepared the day before, are now served. Turkey
is a popular dish. Whole peas and broad beans,
known as *bubb,* boiled in salt water is a favorite
dish. In some localities the Purim gifts are given
out to the members of the family at the *seudah.*

SHUSHAN
PURIM

Because the Jews who lived in Shushan,
capital city of Persia, were permitted
by King Ahasuerus, at Queen Esther's
request, to defend themselves from their enemies also on the fifteenth day of Adar, this day
was named Shushan Purim, the Purim of Shu-

shan. Even to-day the Jewish people are accustomed, in a certain measure, to feasting and rejoicing also on Shushan Purim, which is the second day of Purim mentioned in the Book of Esther.

PRAYER FOR PURIM

"Almighty God and Father, we remember today the darkness and gloom which enveloped our people's life in the past, only to rejoice the more in the great light with which Thou art filling the world, the light of justice and truth, of liberty and love.

"We thank Thee, O Keeper and Guardian of Israel, for the help which Thou didst afford unto our people in the days of Mordecai and Esther, at this season, when Haman, in his malice and revenge, sought to destroy all the Israelites scattered throughout the vast Empire of Persia. But with Thy great and abundant mercy Thou didst frustrate the wicked designs of Haman and caused him to fall into the very snare which he had prepared for Thine innocent children—the persecutor perished, but Thy people were saved and rejoiced.

"In Thine infinite wisdom, O Lord God,

Thou hast chosen a feeble woman to bring salvation to Thy people, that all the world might learn that not by power does man prevail; that that which seems powerless, weak and humble, turns strong, mighty and sublime at Thy will.

"O God, grant me also, that my feeble powers may succeed in doing what is good and useful, that my life may not pass away profitless and fruitless, that my name may become worthy to be praised and blessed by those who live with me and by those who shall live after me. Imbue our hearts with the fidelity of Mordecai and the devotion of Esther, that we may never swerve from the path of duty and loyalty trod by our fathers. Endow us with patience and strength, with purity of heart and unity cf purpose so that we may be worthy to see the forces of darkness, the cruel Amaleks and the vindictive Hamans succumb and vanish from earth, and gladness and strength fill our souls. AMEN."

3. LAG BAOMER

SEPHIRAH DAYS In Palestine, the cereal harvest lasted seven weeks. It began with the harvest of barley, which was celebrated on the second day of Passover by bringing the *omer* offering, and ended with the harvesting of wheat on the fiftieth day after the bringing of the *omer*. This occasion was celebrated by the Festival of Shabuot, the literal meaning of which is *weeks*. (See *Shabuot* for a fuller explanation of this festival).

The seven weeks of the cereal harvest was a season of gladness and joy with the Palestinian farmers, and were so important that they were counted from day to day. These forty-nine days were called *sephirah* (counting) days. Religious Jews all over the world still fulfill the command of the Almighty and count these forty-nine days. Every evening, after the stars have become visible to the naked eye, every Jew in the synagogue rises to his feet and recites a benediction, concluding which he says: "Today is the (mentioning the proper day) day of the *omer*."

In the course of time, the Jews met with persecution and hatred because of their religion, and many gave up their lives for the sake of their people and their Law. One of these unfortunate events, during the Jews' last unsuccessful attempt, under the leadership of Bar Kokhba, to regain their independence, occurred during the *sephirah* days. These days were devoted to the rememberance of these martyrs, and are observed by the Jews not as a joyous season, but as days of mourning. During the *sephirah* days, therefore, no hair may be cut; no marriages may take place; no concerts and no dances may be held.

WHAT IS LAG BAOMER? *Lag* is composed of the two Hebrew letters *gimmel, lammed,* and considered as numerals, these letters signify *thirty-three,* and denote the thirty-third day in the counting of the *omer,* corresponding to the eighteenth day of the Jewish month of Iyyar.

Lag Baomer is observed as a semi-holiday. All rules of mourning are dispensed with on this day. The observance of this semi-holiday has its source in incidents that took place after the bar Kokhba revolution against Rome.

The Rabbis have recorded that, during the

last revolution against the Romans, a dreadful
plague broke out against the disciples of the
great teacher Rabbi Akiba, who was an ardent
supporter of the revolution. This happened during *sphirah* days, and because of the Jews' great
respect for this scholar, these days were declared as days of mourning. On *Lag Baomer*
the epidemic suddenly stopped, and therefore
the sages ordered that day to be observed as
a semi-holiday.

According to another tradition, this semi-
holiday is linked with the great scholar Rabbi
Simeon bar Yohai. After the Roman victory
over Bar Kokhba, the Roman emperor Hadrian
issued cruel decrees against the Jews, aimed at
destroying the Jewish religion and culture. Observance of the Sabbath, and of many other
fundamental precepts and the study of the
Law were forbidden under the penalty of death.
Rabbi Akiba and many other scholars who de-
fied the Roman edict were tortured to death.
Rabbi Simeon bar Yohai, who in defiance to the
Roman edict, continued to instruct his students
in the Law of God, managed to escape.

For twelve long years Simeon bar Yohai
lived with his son Rabbi Eleazar in a cave in
the mountains of Galilee. Fearing the numerous Roman spies in Palestine, Simeon and his

son dared not leave their hideout even to obtain food. A carob-tree and a spring of water miraculously appeared in the cavern. During all the days of their hiding, they ate of the fruit of the carob-tree and drank from the water of the spring. In order to preserve their garments, they sat naked in the sand and their skin became covered with scabs.

At last the prophet Elijah announced to them the death of the emperor and the consequent annulment of the death-sentence against them. Then they left their cave. Rabbi Simeon observed people engaged in farming and other pursuits but neglecting the study of the Law. His anger was aroused by what he saw, and with his angry glances he caused the death of the workers. A voice then descended from heaven ordering father and son to return to the cave, where they remained twelve months longer, until a heavenly voice bade them come forth. The great teacher then settled in Meron, a village near Sefad in Palestine. It is a tradition among the pious Jews that Rabbi Simeon bar Yohai died on *Lag Baomer*, and that before his death he revealed to his disciples the deep secrets which were later found incorporated in the mystic book called "Zohar."

Lag Baomer has been set aside as a special

holiday for school children carrying bows
and arrows, they go with their teachers to nearby woods, and spend the day picnicking and
playing all sorts of games, especially archery.
The bow and arrow are reminiscent of the great
Jewish heroes of the past. At the same time
they arouse hope in the redemption of the Jewish people through the Messiah. For, it is stated
in the Zohar that a bow of many colors will
appear in the sky immediately before the coming of the Messiah.

4. ROSH HODESH

NEW MOON

ROSH
HODESH
OF OLD
Rosh Hodesh, the beginning of the month, had always been considered a semi-holiday among the Hebrews. On this occasion special sacrifices were offered in the Temple at Jerusalem, and trumpets were blown by the Levites.

The New Moon Day had to be accurately fixed, so that the festival days might be exactly determined. During the existence of the second Temple, the calendar was regulated by direct observation. The Sanhedrin, the highest court at Jerusalem, sent witnesses to observe the first appearance of the new moon. A special court, called Bet-Yazek, was established in Jerusalem to hear and examine the witnesses. After the testimony of at least two witnesses had been accepted by the court, the ceremony of announcing the new month was observed by that judicial body in the following manner. The President of the court said: "The new month is proclaimed," and all present said after him, "Proclaimed, proclaimed."

That night, torches and bonfires would be

lit on the highest peak near Jerusalem, as signals
to nearby towns and villages that the new month
had been officially declared. The people on
other peaks, farther away, would in turn light
torches and bonfires as signals to more distant
settlements. Thus the fire signals carried the
news to all the inhabitants of Palestine. Even
the Jews in Babylonia were informed of the
New Moon by relays of torches and bonfires.
The following day was celebrated as *rosh hodesh*,
the beginning of the month.

**ROSH
HODESH
NOW**
After the destruction of the Temple,
the coming of the new moon was
announced, in advance of its appearance, on the Sabbath in the synagogue.
A special prayer was offered expressing the hope
that the new month would be a time of blessing
and good for all Israel, a period characterized
by reverence for God and dread of sin.

The Jewish month, which is regulated by
the lunar and not the solar system, consists
either of twenty-nine or thirty days. When
the previous month has twenty-nine days, only
one day of *rosh hodesh* is observed. When the
preceding month has thirty days, two days of
rosh hodesh are observed, the first day of which
is the thirtieth day of the previous month.

Tradition has made *rosh hodesh* a semi holiday for women. They abstain from sewing and other work which can be postponed. Some men also follow this practice. The meals served on *rosh hodesh* are more festive than on regular week-days.

5. HAMISHAH ASAR BISHEVAT

THE JEWISH ARBOR DAY

Hamishah Asar Bishevat, the fifteenth day of the month of *shevat* (roughly February), is called in the Talmud "the New Year of Trees." In Palestine the day marks the beginning of the season of the budding of the trees. It is generally celebrated by partaking of a variety of sweet fruits, especially Palestinian fruits, such as grapes, raisins, almonds, dates, and figs. A special fruit for the day is the Carob seed, or St. John's bread.

In Palestine, the festival of *Hamishah Asar Bishevat* has assumed a character of great importance; it has become the Jewish Arbor Day, a great national celebration. Since traditionally this has been called a children's holiday, the youngsters in Palestine are given the privilege of planting new trees, amidst a most impressive celebration.

CHAPTER EIGHT

THE FOUR FAST DAYS

A SEASON OF NATIONAL MOURNING

"Rejoice ye with Jerusalem, and be glad with her,
all ye that love her; rejoice for joy with her, all
ye that mourn for her."

(ISAIAH LXVI, 10).

CHAPTER EIGHT

THE FOUR FAST DAYS

A SEASON OF NATIONAL MOURNING

WHAT IS A FAST DAY? Among the Jews fasting, as an expression of grief and extreme sorrow, is very ancient. The Jewish religion adopted it as a sign of remorse and penitence by which forgiveness might be obtained from the God against whom one has sinned. The Jew on public fast days not only commemorates his great national calamities, but also seeks forgiveness for his sins. Implicitly he believes that had not the Jews sinned against their God in the past, they would not have been punished by losing their sanctuary and their land. He therefore fasts in expiation of the sins of his ancient forebears and his own sins as well; for he believes that by purging himself of sin, he will become worthy of national restoration. In other words, the Jewish fast days are national memorial days, recalling the misfortunes of the past; and at the same time serve as a plea to God for the revival of Jewish national existence. The fast days are a means of keeping alive the hope and courage of the Jewish people.

If a fast day occurs on a Sabbath, it is postponed to Sunday, because no fasting is allowed on the Sabbath. (See Yom Kippur, page 212, and Esther's Fast, page 235).

THE FOUR FAST DAYS

All Jewish fast days, except Yom Kippur, are connected with events in Jewish history. Some of these occurrences are recorded in our history books, and others have come down to us by tradition.

Our sages in the Talmud give the following reasons for observing the four fast days:-

(1). The tenth day of the month of Tebet is observed as a fast day, because on that day Nebuchadnezzar, the king of Babylon, approached the city of Jerusalem and laid siege to it.

(2). The seventeenth day of Tammuz is observed as a fast day, because four sorrowful events occurred on this day: (a). The tablets, on which the Ten Commandments were inscribed, were broken by Moses, when he descended from Mount Sinai and found that the Israelites had made a golden calf which they had worshiped. (b). The regular daily sacrifice in the Temple was abolished. (c). Apostemus burned the Torah and introduced an idol in the Temple. (d). The Romans broke into the city of Jerusalem during the existence of the second Temple.

(3). The ninth day of Ab is observed as a fast day, because five tragic events occurred on that day: (a). When the Israelites were in the wilderness, after their departure from Egypt, Moses sent scouts to explore Canaan, the land of their promise. On the ninth day of Ab the scouts returned with discouraging reports, and as told in the Bible: "All the congregation lifted up their voices and cried." God thereupon decreed that those men who had left Egypt should die during their wanderings of forty years in the wilderness and not enter the promised land. (b). The first Temple was destroyed on this day by the Babylonians. (c). And the second Temple by the Romans. (d). Jerusalem was ploughed over with ploughshares by the Roman procurator Tinnius Rufus. (e). The city of Bethar was conquered by the

Roman legions during the Bar Kokhba revolution.

4. The third day of Tishri is a fast which commemorates the murder of Gedaliah, the son of Achikam. After the destruction of the first Temple, the Babylonian king Nebuchadnezzar left a small number of farmers in Palestine, and appointed Gedaliah as their governor. These farmers, under the leadership of the prophet Jeremiah and the governor Gedaliah, began to rebuild the ruined land. Unfortunately Gedaliah was assassinated by traitors, and the remnant of Jews left in Palestine were either exiled or slain by the Babylonians. Thus the last hope of Israel vanished.

THE THREE WEEKS The three weeks, between the seventeenth day of Tammuz and the ninth day of Ab, are a period of mourning in remembrance of the great misfortunes that befell the Jews many centuries ago. They pray to their Father in heaven to free them from their heartless oppressors, and to bring them to their coveted land of Palestine.

During these days the Jews observe some of the rules that apply to those who mourn the death of their next of kin: They perform no marriages; they play no musical instruments;

they do not purchase new garments; and they do not have their hair trimmed.

THE NINE DAYS From the first to the ninth day of the month of Ab, the grief of the Jews grows deeper, and they observe even more stringent rules of mourning to express their sorrow. Joy and merriment is avoided as much as possible: they drink no wine during these nine days, except on the Sabbath; they do not wash their clothes; they do not bathe even in cold water; and take no walks for pleasure's sake.

SABBATH HAZON The Sabbath that occurs during the first nine days of Ab, is known as *Sabbath Hazon,* because the weekly portion of the prophets which is read in the synagogue at the Sabbath morning service — the first chapter of Isaiah — begins with the word *hazon,* the vision of. This chapter is read with the same traditional plaintive melody as that of Lamentations read on the Ninth of Ab.

In this chapter, the prophet, in scathing terms, reproaches the Jewish people for their backslidings. He prophesies that very evil days will come to punish their sins, but ends with words of consolation.

[259]

THE NINTH OF AB On all other fast days food may be had during the night preceding the feast, but no food may be had on the night preceding the Ninth of Ab. The meal before this fast must be ended before sunset. At this meal some orthodox Jews eat an egg, symbolic of mourning, and add a little ashes to their food, indicating the reducing of the Temple to ashes.

On the Ninth of Ab, every Jew observes all rules of mourning. In the evening, he goes to the synagogue, removes his shoes if made of leather, and sits either on a low stool or on the floor, while the reader in measured, plaintive, traditional tones chants Lamentations. This is one of the books of the Bible written by the prophet Jeremiah who lived during the destruction of the first Temple. In beautiful and poetic words this prophet mourns the sad lot of the Jew.

Returning home from the synagogue, the Jew does not offer the usual greeting to his family. Sorrow, gloom and sadness reign in the house. Even sleeping quarters are made less comfortable than on ordinary nights: some remove the pillows from under their heads, while others sleep on the floor.

In the morning, the Jew does not wash or

bathe in warm water, but simply wets his fingers and eyes with cold water, not using any soap; nor does he massage himself. He does not greet the members of his family as usual, but silently goes to the synagogue to offer prayers.

In the synagogue, the worshipers again sit either on low stools or on the floor, pray and again listen to the reading of Lamentations. The prayers ended, the Jew returns home, without greeting any one either in the synagogue or on his way home.

The Jew abstains from eating and drinking all day until after the appearance of the stars; he does not greet people and does not wear leather shoes all day; until noon, he does not sit on regular chairs or benches, and he does not engage in any work.

After the morning service, some Jews make it a custom to visit the cemetery.

(*An appropriate prayer for the Ninth of Ab.*)

"Merciful Father, with deep grief do we this day remember the fatal day on which the enemy entered Thy fortress Zion, and Thy Sanctuary became a prey to consuming flames. The glorious Temple upon Moriah's proud heights where the children of Israel praised Thy holy name when all nations worshiped despicable idols, and the holy vessels it contained, were destroyed by the enemy. The sweet melodious voices of the Levites and their musical instruments were silenced, and only the outcries of agony and lamentation were heard in the midst of Thy Holy City Jerusalem. Alas, heavy and bitter affliction didst Thou, O Lord, impose upon the children of Israel.

"And since that terrible calamity for the children of Israel, Thy people, O Lord, throughout the long bitter exile, wherever their fugitive feet trod, found the yoke of oppression, the curse of hatred, the poisonous arrow of calumny, and many thousands of their sons and daughters were forced to sacrifice their fortunes and their lives in their struggle to sanctify Thy holy name and Thy Torah. In all these bitter trials, Thy people recognized Thy paternal guidance, and lost neither hope nor faith in Thee.

"Grant, O merciful God, that Thy people continue to bear their trials and tribulations with courage and fortitude, and that their faith in Thee and in Thy promise of redemption shall never be shaken. Grant, O Lord, that their mourning may end everywhere, wherever they may yet sigh and groan under the yoke of hatred and persecution; open the eyes of all nations who still regard the sons of Israel as rejected from before Thy presence, and by Thy merciful acts convince them that Israel is still Thy beloved people who follow the precepts of Thy Law at the risk of their very lives.

"O God, have mercy upon Israel, Thy people, upon Jerusalem, Thy Holy City, and upon Thy Holy Temple, and rebuild them speedily in our days. May the land of our fathers, the land of Israel, be a home for the persecuted and exiled of our people. May the time come when out of Zion shall come forth enduring values and doctrines which will influence the hearts of men everywhere so that they will outlaw the dominion of might and arrogance, and acclaim Thy rule for righteous living.

"O send the Messiah, Thy anointed, speedily in our days. AMEN."

SABBATH NAHAMU   The Sabbath following the nine days of Ab is called *Sabbath Nahamu,* the Sabbath of comfort, because we read at the morning service in the synagogue for the weekly reading from the Prophets the fortieth chapter of Isaiah, commencing with the words *nahamu, nahamu,* comfort ye, comfort ye. Thus again after the period of mourning, the Jew is imbued with words of hope and consolation for a bright future. The Jew has never lost confidence in the help of God and in the final victory of justice and truth.

CHAPTER NINE

JEWISH FAMILY LIFE

"Every wise woman buildeth her house, but the foolish plucketh it down with her own hands."

(PROVERBS XIV, 1).

CHAPTER NINE

JEWISH FAMILY LIFE

MARRIAGE A SACRED DUTY Among the Jews marriage is not a mere civil contract; it is a sacred duty and a great privilege. "It is not good for the man to be alone," were God's words concerning the first man, Adam. "I must make a help-mate for him." To point out to all generations to come that the bond of marriage, the union between husband and wife, is natural and not artificial, the Almighty took a rib from Adam's body, fashioned it in the shape of a woman and gave it to him as a gift. The Almighty then decreed that man and wife must become one unit, "one flesh."

Jewish legend still further embellished this first bond of human marriage. It tells that the Almighty Himself acted as best man at the wedding. He bestowed grace and sweetness upon the first bride, and adorned her, before presenting her to Adam, the first bride-groom. He then turned to the heavenly host of angels and said: "Come let us perform friendly service to Adam and his help-mate on this occasion; friendliness is by far more pleasing to Me than sacrifices offered upon the altar."

The angels accordingly assembled around the marriage canopy, and the Almighty Himself, acting as celebrant, pronounced the blessings upon the bridal couple. The angels then danced and played musical instruments before the newly-weds, and thus, accompanied by heavenly voices and angelic music, the first couple were led into the ten bridal chambers of gold, pearls and precious stones, which the Almighty Himself had prepared for them.

SANCTIFICATION Betrothal, in Hebrew law, is called *kiddushin,* meaning *sanctification.* In the Jewish religious concept, a woman by her marriage becomes the sanctified possession of her husband, and as such she is forbidden to all others. That is why the voice of the Almighty thundered on Mount Sinai in the seventh commandment: "Thou shalt not commit adultery." A married woman must be faithful to her husband, and a married man must be faithful to his wife.

As among most nations of antiquity, adultery committed by a married woman was considered by the Jews to be a grave offense punishable, according to the divine command, by death. Both the woman guilty of adultery and her paramour, are to be punished with death.

According to the sages of the Talmud, the union of every couple to be married is chosen in heaven by the Almighty Himself. Furthermore, they maintain that forty days before a child is born its mate is determined by heavenly decree. The breaking of this sacred bond by infidelity was therefore so severely punished.

DEVOTION TO HUSBAND The Jewish people have always been known for their devotion in marriage. A classic example of that devotion was shown almost three thousand years ago by Princess Michal, the daughter of King Saul. She risked her life to save the life of her husband David, who later succeeded her father Saul to the throne of Israel.

Saul, the first king of Israel, had become jealous of his son-in-law whose heroic deeds had practically made him the idol of the Jews. By killing the giant Goliath, David had saved the people of Israel from their enemies, the Philistines. King Saul knew that not his son Jonathan, but David would succeed him to the throne of Israel. He therefore made many attempts on David's life.

One day King Saul ordered his servants to go down to David's house and kill him. Princess Michal, having discovered the plot, warned David: "If you save not your life to-night, to-morrow you will be slain." She insisted that he leave the house that night. David escaped by a rope which she lowered from an upper window. Michal then placed a figure in David's bed, at the head of which she put a quilt of goat's hair, and she covered it with a cloth. When the king's men arrived, Michal said: "David is sick in bed." When the king received the message, he ordered: "Bring him up to me in his bed, that I may slay him."

It was then that the king's messengers discovered the hoax. Princess Michal was thereupon summoned before the king who sternly said: "Why have you deceived me thus, and let my enemy escape?"

Michal knew the blind hatred and the fierce fury of her royal father, and she had to lie to save her life: "He said to me: Let me go; why should I kill you?"

STATUS OF WIFE Among other nations of antiquity, a wife was considered chattel, the possession of her husband. The social status of the Jewish wife was one of equality with her husband. A family-loving people, the Jews maintained a reverent attitude toward womankind. Not the husband but the law determined to the minutest detail the personal and social status as well as the dower rights of the wife.

Even in the earliest days of Jewish history, the woman was qualified to attain the highest social position, even that of judge and prophetess of God. Miriam, the sister of Moses and Aaron, was crowned with the title prophetess by the Almighty Himself. Deborah, Huldah and others were worthy of receiving God's word. And women were eligible to occupy the throne of the Jewish kingdom.

INFLUENCE OF WIFE "It is all up to the woman," say our Talmudic sages; for she can make her husband and children happy and her home blessed with peace. She can influence her husband and children to be honest and God-fearing. She can bring a sense of mildness, courtesy, and kindness to the members of her family. On the other hand, she may become an evil influence in her household. It is for this reason that our Talmudic sages regarded the acquisition of a virtuous wife as one of the greatest blessings. "Who is rich?" say the Rabbis; "he who has a wife whose deeds are noble." And the Rabbis of the Talmud added that a man would prefer all the evils of the world to that one evil—a quarrelsome and spiteful wife.

DUTY TO CHILDREN Who can fathom the love of a Jewish mother for her children? Her devotion for them is so great that she often neglects her own life for theirs. She finds her own happiness in the happiness of her children.

However, every Jewish mother must utilize such love in influencing her children, especially when they are still young, to grow up good Jews and honest men. She must impress upon her children that there is something higher and nobler in life than mere earthly pleasures. This is well illustrated in the biblical story of Isaac's wife Rebecca. Rebecca preferred her younger son Jacob, a simpleton who spent most of his time in his tent, to her first-born Esau who spent his time hunting in the fields. She knew that it would be Jacob who would carry on the religion of his fathers.

The Jewish mother must teach her children to choose the right companions in life. She must be extremely careful to watch and observe the type of friends with whom her children are associating. Our first Jewish mother Sarah gave a splendid example of such teaching.

Sarah's husband, Abraham, had a son by Hagar named Ishmael. Because Ishmael was quarrelsome, the inheritor of a pagan culture that exalted bloodshed and dissension, Sarah did not want him under the same roof with her own son Isaac. She feared Ishmael would prove a bad influence upon Isaac. Abraham, however, hesitated to send Ishmael away; his paternal love was strong. But the Almighty Himself came to Sarah's aid. He warned Abraham to heed Sarah's wish, for Isaac was destined to carry on his father's faith.

HEBREW TRAINING Unfortunately, many of our Jewish mothers neglect the Jewish education of their children. They begin to send their sons to a Hebrew School or engage a Hebrew teacher for them, only in order to prepare them for their Bar Mitzvah. Such brief preparatory training is neither enduring nor effectual. These untrained children grow up to be total strangers among their Jewish brethren, unacquainted with their mode of life and manner of thought. This lack of understanding necessarily creates a gap between parents and children; they do not understand one another; and no real relationship exists between them.

For your children, boys and girls, to belong to your people and yourself, they must be given a genuine Jewish education. Send them to a Hebrew School when they are young. Let them gradually learn to understand our sacred traditions and glorious past, that they may be prepared to perform their duties. The Jewish religion will teach them to respect their people, their forefathers, and you as their mother. A genuine friendship will then exist between you and your children which will never be estranged; for, your child will become a link of that long chain of Jewish generations who valiantly suffered and fought to maintain their noble ideals.

BIRTH OF A CHILD Upon giving birth to a child, every Jewish woman must pray to God, expressing her gratitude for having spared her life and her appreciation for the new-born child. The following is an appropriate prayer for the occasion:

"Almighty God, we thank Thee fervently for the child with which Thou hast blessed our home. Accept our grateful prayers, that through the clouds of anxiety has come the light of a new joy, by which our spirits are exalted and our marriage bond is sanctified anew.

"Thou art the Author of life, and in Thy grace and love hast bestowed upon us the gift of this new life. In reverence and joy do we receive this sacred trust. May we be found worthy of Thy favor, O Lord God. Help us to fulfill our duties as parents wisely and faithfully, whatever may be the sacrifice.

"Let Thy blessing rest upon our child. Keep him (her) in life, and sustain him (her) in health, that we may rear him (her) for loving service to others and devotion to Thee. Mayest Thou guard him (her) against every evil and keep him (her) from every danger. AMEN."

CIRCUMCISION When a son is eight days old, he must be inducted into the covenant of Abraham, by being circumcised. Our father Abraham was the first to receive God's command concerning circumcision: "This is My covenant, which you shall keep, between Me and you and your seed after you: every male-child among you shall be circumcised. He that is eight days old shall be circumcised among you, every man child throughout all generations."

This surgical operation is recommended by physicians today for purely hygienic reasons. But among the Jews circumcision has a moral value. By being circumcised, the child becomes a member of the Jewish family, a son of Abraham, and a party to the covenant made between the Almighty and the children of Israel. By this, the child is dedicated to the precepts of the Lord and to His moral teachings, so that he can devote himself in his riper years to the cause of his God and of his people.

On the occasion of circumcision of her son, the mother should offer the following prayer:

"O Lord God, in accordance with Thy command, we have this day caused our newborn son to be brought into the holy covenant of our father Abraham. We have brought this sacrifice with joy and gladness of heart to do Thy will.

"Therefore, I beseech Thee, O merciful Father, to help us guide our son upon the path of virtue and righteousness. Grant us strength and health so that we may be able to raise our son and teach him to fulfill Thy holy precepts. May this infant grow up to be a faithful follower of Thy Torah, a dutiful son to his parents, and a leader among his people Israel.

"When he sins before Thee, O Lord, be mindful of the blood we willingly and joyfully shed this day, and forgive his folly. Purify his heart that he may serve Thee in truth, and be merciful unto him.

"O Lord God, grant my husband and me the happiness of seeing this tender infant grow up into manhood. May we live to see him grow up as a faithful Jew and an honorable man. Put into the heart of my son the love and fear of Thee, that he may consecrate his life to Thy service and glorify Thy holy name in the eyes of all men.

"Let the words of my mouth and the meditation of my heart be acceptable in Thy sight, O Lord God, my Shield and my Redeemer. Be our support when grief silences our voice, and our comfort when woe bends our spirit. AMEN."

NAMING OF BOYS At the circumcision ceremony, the child is named, usually after a departed relative either on the father's or on the mother's side. When naming the child, remember that the Hebrew names are beautiful and meaningful. Do not try to change a Hebrew name into a gentile one. Gentiles of great prominence were not ashamed to assume Hebrew biblical names. Why, then, should you be ashamed to call your children by such names? By adopting gentile names, you show that you lack a feeling of self-respect, of spiritual and national independence. What a pity that most of our brothers and sisters do not realize it!

NAMING OF GIRLS Girls are generally named at the synagogue on the first Sabbath after they are born. On that day the father usually attends the morning services at the synagogue, and when he is called up to say the benediction over the Torah, the newly-born girl is named by the *hazzan* (cantor).

REDEMPTION OF THE FIRST-BORN (PIDYON HA-BEN) All first-born males of men as well as of animals, belonged to God, among the children of Israel. Such was God's decree. First-born males were to devote themselves to the active service of God, while first-born *kosher* animals were to be given to the priest. The first-born of asses were redeemed or repurchased by a lamb.

By the Law of God, however, the first-born sons may be formally redeemed or repurchased from the priest by paying five *shekels*—approximately three dollars. This religious ceremony of redemption of the first-born takes place when the boy is fully thirty days old. Only the first-born son of the mother must be redeemed but not of the father. If a man, who has never before been married, marries a woman who has had children by another husband, their son is not to be redeemed.

Again, the child must be actually the first-born. If the mother gave birth to a daughter before the birth of a son, he requires no redemption.

If the mother is the daughter of either a Kohen or a Levi, her first-born son need not be redeemed.

The ceremony of redemption takes place in the following manner: A *Kohen*, a descendant of the priestly tribe of Aaron, redeems the child at the father's request, by receiving five *shekels* as redemption money. This ceremony is generally accompanied by an elaborate feast to which at least ten male adult persons are invited. On this occasion, the mother should recite the following prayer:

"Our God and God of our fathers, I thank Thee from the bottom of my heart for Thy great mercy in granting us life and health to reach this joyous occasion of redeeming my first-born son.

"In accordance with Thy command, we have redeemed our son from the *Kohen* that he may from now on be ours, ours forever. May it be Thy gracious will that we be worthy to guide our son to be devoted to Thee, to Thy Law and to Thy people Israel. Bestow Thy heavenly blessing upon our house and upon our infant, and may we always find grace in Thy sight, our Shield and our Redeemer.

"O Lord, as we redeemed our tender son this day, so mayest Thou in Thy mercy ever redeem him from all trouble, pain, and anxiety. Grant that he ever be guided by the commandments of Thy Torah and by the shining light of Thy holy Law.

"Praised be Thou, O Lord, for this happy day that Thou hast granted us. May our hearts be as altars of thanksgiving from which rise offerings of praise unto Thee. May we show our gratitude by deeds of kindness, so that other hearts may rejoice with ours. And mayest Thou be with us in days to come, keeping us faithful unto all the duties of life, and help us to be strong in trial and temptation.

"Guide us, O Lord, by the light of Thy counsel, and let us ever find rest in Thee, who art our Shield and our Redeemer. AMEN."

BAR MITZVAH
(CONFIRMATION) The thirteenth birthday of a Jewish boy is known as "Bar Mitzvah Day." On this day of confirmation the boy assumes the obligation of observing all the commandments incumbent upon all Jews. From that day, the boy is considered a full-fledged member of the Jewish community. He is qualified to participate as one of the ten male adults in a *minyan*, the minimum congregational quorum required to hold communal or synagogue worship.

From the day of his *bar mitzvah*, the boy must also lay *tephilin* at the morning prayers on weekdays. Each box of the *tephilin* contains pieces of parchment on which are written some passages from the Holy Scriptures. One of the *tephilin* is worn on the left arm opposite the heart, and the other on the head above the forehead, in order that they may influence our hearts and minds to follow the Law of God, and to love and obey Him with all our heart and soul. The *tephilin* further reminds the Jew that the Lord delivered his forebears from Egypt, from bondage and slavery, and inspire him with the hope that the Lord will deliver him from his present exile and bring him back to his land, the land of Israel.

The following is an appropriate prayer for

a mother to offer on her child's day of confirmation:

"Praised be Thou, O Lord God, for this
happy day which Thou hast granted to us. Thou
hast graciously given us life and health to edu-
cate and guide our beloved son with paternal
love and tenderness; to provide him with all that
he was in need of, and to prepare him for this
most solemn day of his life on which he is received into the congregation of Israel to participate in the performance and fulfillment of
Thy holy laws and commandments.

"O Lord God, grant that the religion to
which my son has dedicated himself this day
shall ever fill his heart. May his soul be illum-
ined by the light of truth, and may his heart
be inspired with all that is noble and great.
May his spirit be strengthened and encouraged
for the struggles against the dangers and temp-
tations of life, against the power of sin, passions,
and allurements. Grant that this tender child
may grow up and mature to be a strong in-
strument of salvation for his people and his
country, to glorify his faith, and promote all
that is good and useful on earth.

"Hearken, O God, unto the fervent prayer
of a mother's heart. O strengthen my son's
body and make his understanding mature. Pre-

serve the purity of his morals, the innocence of his soul, and the peace of his heart, as they now fill his youthful being. Strengthen his determination to be faithful unto Thee.

"O God, grant that for a long time to come I may delight in my son with the gratification of a mother's love. Grant that his parents may for many years to come guide him upon the path of Thy law, and may Thy gracious favor continue to bless our home. May Thy holy light shine in our abode, the light of love and truth, the light of peace and goodwill. AMEN."

CONFIRMATION OF GIRLS

The confirmation of girls generally takes place on the Shabuot festival at the morning services in the synagogue. (See page 173).

INTER-MARRIAGES

The Jews were admonished by the Almighty in the Torah: "You shall not intermarry with them (the heathens). Your daughters you shall not give to their sons, and your sons you shall not give to their daughters." Intermarriage was forbidden lest it introduce into the life of the Jew ideals and cultures directly opposed to the teachings of God.

THE PURITY LAWS

WHY PURITY LAWS? The Jewish religion governs and regulates the physical relations of man and wife. It takes precautions to safeguard the health of the Jewish woman and the health of the offspring. Chief of these precautions is the law that dictates a cessation of sexual relations for a certain number of days each month.

These periodic separations, as required by the Jewish law, have the sanction of modern medical authority. Noted scientists support the biblical law which forbids sexual intercourse during the woman's menstrual periods. They maintain that the adherence to this law by the Jews was the direct cause for the sturdiness of the Jewish stock.

There is also a moral and spiritual significance to this law. Since, among the Jews, women enjoy equality with men, they must not be considered as having been created by the Almighty for the purpose of satisfying male lust. They were created by Him to be helpers to their husbands, to raise families, and to enjoy all the freedom that the Almighty saw fit to bestow upon men.

Men, among most nations of the world,

were brutal in their conduct towards their wives.
Women had no say in the matter of their mari-
tal relations, but were treated like slaves. The
Almighty, to put an end to this condition,
endowed marriage with a touch of holiness. He
decreed that the husband, under the threat of
the severest penalty that can be meted out to
men, must abstain from his lust and control
his desires during certain periods of his wife's
life, because she is not at his beck and call.

The Jewish woman should not ignore the
divine rights given her by the Almighty. Adherence to God's law safeguards her health and
that of her offspring, serves as a moral disci-
pline, and also begets mutual love and reverence.

The purity laws have been observed by
the Jews for thousands of years with excellent
results, and should therefore be respected by
modern women. To follow the Jewish traditions, one must abide by all the laws and regulations embracing the biblical and the Talmudic
requirements.

LAWS TO BE OBSERVED DURING THE MENSTRUAL PERIOD A woman who observes a dis-
charge of blood from her womb,
whether it be during the time of
her regular monthly period or not,
is considered menstrually unclean. Both man and woman who have sexual

intercourse after the menstrual flow has begun
are punishable, according to the Law of Moses,
by "being cut off from their people," and the
punishment for caressing one another is lashing,
according to Maimonides.

The woman becomes menstrually unclean
even when the issue of blood has resulted from
an accident. She must count seven days of
purification after this (see page 292), and then
take the proper bath of immersion (*mikvah*).
(See page 296).

If she has not felt the blood issuing from
her womb, but finds a stain of blood upon her
body, undergarments, sheet, or any other place,
and she cannot attribute its appearance to any
other cause than to an issue from her womb,
she is menstrually unclean.

A woman who finds a stain which is neither
exactly red nor exactly white, should consult
a competent Rabbi for an opinion.

If a woman feels that she has begun to
menstruate but cannot find visible proof, she
is nevertheless considered menstrually unclean.
But if she discovers a white secretion from her
body unstained with red, she is considered clean.

Not only is sexual intercourse forbidden
during the menstrual period, but also any conversation or act leading to sexual intercourse.

The husband may not come in contact with his wife's body—not even with her little finger; he is not allowed to hand anything to her, nor to receive anything from her; he is not permitted to drink whatever she has left in her cup, although she may drink whatever is left over in his cup.

They are not permitted to sleep in the same bed. They are not allowed to swing in the same swing.

Our sages permit the woman to powder, paint and adorn herself during her menstrual period.

She is not permitted, in the presence of her husband, to pour a cup of wine for him, nor bring it to him, nor set it before him on the table. She is not allowed to make his bed while he is present.

If her husband is sick and there is none but her to attend to him, she may do so, but she must be careful not to come in contact with his body. She may, if necessary, raise him up, lay him down, and support him. Even greater care is required when washing his face, hands, and feet, and making his bed in his presence. One should avoid such things whenever possible.

All of the foregoing laws, pertaining to abstinence from acts of intimacy, apply not only to the actual days of the menstrual period but apply as well to the seven days of purification after the flow has ceased. (See page 292).

HOW THE MENSES ARE REGULATED If menstruation occurs on the same day of the month for three consecutive months, then that day is to be considered as the regular time of the menses. This way of reckoning is termed, "menses regulated by diurnal symptoms."

Most women, however, reckon their regular time of the menses by the number of days which elapse between periods. Equal lapses of time for three consecutive months establish the date of the menses. This is termed, "menses regulated by intermittent diurnal symptoms."

Those women who are unable to reckon the date of the menses by either of these methods, must depend upon bodily symptoms. Some women before menstruation, yawn drowsily, or sneeze, or feel a pain in the region of the naval or the womb, or have an attack of chills and fever, or feel their hair bristle, or their head and limbs grow heavy with weariness. If any one of these symptoms occurs immediately before the menses for *three periods in succession*, it may serve to establish the date of the menses. This is termed, "menses regulated by bodily symptoms." A single yawn or sneeze, however, cannot be considered a symptom, as this might happen purely as a common coincidence.

Some women establish their menstrual terms by a combination of diurnal, or intermittent diurnal symptoms, with bodily symptoms. Such a combination occurring *three times in succession* may establish the menstrual date. This is termed, "menses regulated by combined symptoms."

A woman whose periods are regular is presumed to be clean at all times except during her menstrual period, and she need not examine herself either before or after having sexual intercourse. But a woman whose terms are irrgeular must examine herself before and after intercourse to ascertain whether or not she is clean.

THE SEPARATION BEFORE THE MENSTRUAL TERM It is the duty of the husband and wife to separate from each other immediately before the wife's menstrual periods. According to a Talmudic authority, Rabba, the husband should separate himself from his wife twelve hours before her period. If menstruation is expected towards the end of the day, they are to cease cohabitation from the beginning of the day. And if the flow is expected in the morning — whether it begins or not—they are not to have sexual intercourse at all that day. Conversely, if it is expected any time during the night, they are forbidden one another that entire night.

Some authorities are of the opinion that the period of separation is twenty-four hours: that is, if her terms occur at night, she is forbidden to her husband also the whole of the preceding day; and if it occurs by day, she is also forbidden to her husband the whole of the preceding night. It is proper to adopt this custom. If, however, the husband is about to start on a journey, or if he has just returned from one, or if the wife has performed the ceremony of immersion on the previous night, they need not adhere to the above custom.

A woman after the first three months of her pregnancy and a woman who nurses a child, are presumed to have ceased their flow and need not be concerned about their terms. When the period of her nursing is over, a woman must resume observing her former terms. If she reckoned her term by a given day of the month, she must expect its recurrence on that date; if her term was reckoned by intermittent diurnal symptoms, she cannot predict the date of its recurrence. Once it occurs she must then expect the customary interval between periods.

BIRTH AND MISCARRIAGE A woman who has given birth is unclean as of childbirth whether or not the child was born alive. This is true even in the event of an abortive and even if no flow of blood was present. According to law, a woman who has born a son is considered unclean for seven days on account of birth, after which she must count seven clean days and perform the ceremony of immersion. If she has born a daughter, she is considered unclean for fourteen days on account of birth, after which she must count seven clean days before performing the ceremony of immersion. In some communities the custom prevails that women do not perform the ceremony of immersion until forty days after the birth of a son and eighty days after the birth of a daughter. Wherever this is an accepted custom it must not be disregarded, for surely there is a reason for its acceptance.

A woman who has suffered a miscarriage after the embryo has been formed is considered unclean as of a female birth. She should, however, consult a competent Rabbi, for in some instances leniency is proper.

If some time after miscarrying a male child, a woman drops the after-birth, since it is likely that the after-birth is also that of a female child, she is unclean as of female birth. In this case, too, it is best to seek the opinion of a competent Rabbi.

If a woman is certain that she has not conceived, and she performed the ceremony of immersion, and if within forty days she has an abortion, she need not deem it a birth, because the embryo is not formed in less than forty days. She is, however, menstrually unclean, even if she has not perceived any blood; it is presumed that there was a flow of blood which was not noticed, for it is impossible that the womb should be opened without blood.

THE SEVEN DAYS OF PURIFICATION The period during which husband and wife must be separated comprises at least twelve days, of which the first five are the days of the menses and the remaining seven the days of purification.

After perceiving blood, the woman must count no less than five days of impurity, that is, four days in addition to the one on which she has perceived the flow. Even if she noticed it at the end of the day, as long as it was before sunset this day is counted as one of the five. It is immaterial how much blood was seen. A drop or even a stain is sufficient. On the other hand if she continues to bleed the entire five days, so long as the flow ceases before sunset on the fifth day, her period of menses is over and she may immediately begin the seven days of purification as prescribed.

On the fifth day, towards sunset, she should carefully examine herself to ascertain whether or not the flow has completely ceased. If not, she should repeat this examination every day at this time until she learns definitely that the flow has ceased. This fact has to be established beyond doubt, and not until then can the seven days of purification be commenced. In no case, however, can the seven days of purification be commenced before the expiration of the five days after the perception of the first flow.

It is important to note that among the Jews the evening always counts as the beginning of the day. Thus, if the menses began, for instance, on Saturday evening, it is counted as Sunday, and the fifth day for the examination is Thursday before sunset.

The menses over, the woman should prepare herself for the seven days of purification. She should wash her body, and put on clean white undergarments. Her other garments also should be clean. At night she should spread a clean white sheet on her bed, and the pillows and the bed-covering should also be clean. Then on the following morning she should begin to count the seven clean days.

During the seven days she must examine herself twice daily, once in the morning and once near sunset. Should she through negligence examine herself only once on the first day and once on the seventh day, it is proper to be lenient about it. But she should never neglect these examinations knowingly.

The examination must be made by the light of the day and not by artificial light at dusk or at night.

If she should find a stain or a flow of blood during the seven days, she need not wait another five days, but only until the sunset after the flow has ceased. She may then put on clean linens, and on the following day she may begin to count the seven clean days anew.

PREPARING FOR THE IMMERSION Before sunset of the seventh day of purification, she should carefully wash her entire body with warm water until she is perfectly spotless, and thoroughly cleanse and comb her hair. It

is necessary that the combing take place before
night-fall.

Before the ritual immersion takes place, the
whole body should receive the minutest attention. The nails of the fingers and toes must
be trimmed neatly; artificial teeth, rings, ear-
rings, bandages, plaster, and all other foreign
bodies must be removed; so must stains of dye,
tar, adhesion of dough, clay, or any other substance be removed. The coloring used by women
on their faces, hands, and hair need not be
removed.

Really pious women avoid the handling of
any clammy substance, which might stick to
the fingers, on the day before the immersion.
Some women abstain from eating meat or fish,
particles of which might remain between the
teeth.

If the time for the ritual immersion falls
on Sabbath eve, the preparatory washing should
be done in the daytime, because no warm bath
may be taken on the Sabbath. The same rule
applies to the day preceding a festival.

With regard to lighting the Sabbath
candles, it is best to take the preparatory bath
at home, light the candles before sunset, and
thereafter take the bath of immersion. If this

be impossible, then the husband should light the candles; and if this, too, is impossible, then she should light the candles while it is still daytime and say the necessary benediction over them, but she should say or think while lighting them that she does not, by that act, take upon herself the obligations due to the sanctity of the Sabbath. This is valid only in case of emergency.

If the ritual bath is to be taken on the close of the Sabbath or Festival, a competent Rabbi should be consulted as to when and how the preparations for the immersion should take place.

THE RITUAL BATH OF IMMERSION (MIKVAH) The Hebrew word *mikvah* signifies a gathering of water. Hundreds of years ago our sages ordained that the ritual bath of immersion must be taken in a natural gathering of water; hence an ordinary bath does not satisfy the religious requirements of a *mikvah*. The ritualistic usage of the *mikvah* goes back to the very early age when Israel was first taught by Moses the great principles of moral purity and religious sanctity.

The ritual bath should take place—preferably without delay—at the end of the seven days of purification, after the stars have become visible to the naked eye. Under no circumstances may it take place before nightfall.

Usually an attendant at the bath, a Jewish woman, stands at the side of the woman during the immersion to assist her and to see that the immersion is ritually carried out. The attendant should make certain that not a single strand of the woman's hair remains floating above the water. The attendant should not hold the woman while she is under water, because nothing must intervene between the water and the body. In case of emergency, however, the attendant may hold her only after immersing her own hands in the *mikvah,* and then only with a moderate grasp.

The entire body and hair must be bare and immersed at one time.

During the immersion, the woman should not stand erect, for in that position certain parts of her body would not come in contact with the water; nor should she stoop too low, lest certain parts of her body be pressed too close together; but should stoop slightly. It is not necessary for her to distend her thighs nor to extend her arms, but arms and legs should be relaxed as in walking.

She should neither open her mouth nor should she shut it more tightly than necessary.

Her lips should be fairly close to one another. If strands of hair are in her mouth when immersing, the immersion is not valid, as the water would not reach her hair.

She should not keep her eyes tightly closed, because then wrinkles are formed underneath them, nor should her eyes be dilated, as wrinkles are thus formed above them; but she should keep them slightly closed.

She should not stand on anything but the bottom of the pool, during the immersion.

After she has performed the immersion in the proper manner, and while she is still standing in the water, she should fold her arms together on her body, and without looking into the water, pronounce the following benediction:

בָּרוּךְ אַתָּה יְהוָֹה אֱלֹהֵינוּ, מֶלֶךְ הָעוֹלָם, אֲשֶׁר קִדְּשָׁנוּ בְּמִצְוֹתָיו, וְצִוָּנוּ עַל מִצְוַת טְבִילָה.

"Barukh attah adonai, elohenu melekh haolam, asher kidshanu bemitzvotav, vetzivanu al mitzvat tebilah."

"Praised be Thou, O Lord our God, King of the universe, who hast sanctified us by Thy commandments, and hast bidden us to observe the ceremony of immersion."

[298]

She may, if necessary, be prompted by the attendant in pronouncing the benediction.

Some women immerse themselves again after pronouncing the benediction. This is a proper custom. Those who do so must take heed that the second immersion, too, be properly carried out.

THE BRIDE It is the duty of every Jewish mother to teach her betrothed daughter the duties and responsibilities of wifehood. If the bride has no mother, then some true friend should undertake that task. The bride should also know the respect due her by her bridegroom, in accordance with the Jewish law.

With few exceptions, all the laws pertaining to a woman in her periods apply to a bride at her marriage.

Every bride is, according to the Jewish law, in the state of impurity as that of a woman in her monthly periods.

Before the date upon which the marriage has been fixed, therefore, she must count and observe seven days of purification (see page 292). This should be so arranged that the seventh day of purification should occur a day or two before the wedding, but under no circumstances more than four days before.

A woman should not be married before purifying herself of her uncleanliness, unless the circumstances are such that the wedding cannot be delayed.

A bride must take the ritual bath of immersion on the seventh or eighth day of purification. She may attend to this sacred duty even in the daytime. But if she takes the ritual bath after the wedding ceremony, it cannot be taken in the daytime.

A virgin bride, after her first sexual intercourse, is considered unclean, as if she were in a menstrual period. For the first four days she is in a state of absolute impurity, after which she must observe seven days of purification. She must then take the ritual bath of immersion, before she may have sexual intercourse again.

It is customary for the bride and the bridegroom to fast on their wedding day, to obtain forgiveness for their sins. They are to fast until after the nuptial ceremony only. If the ceremony is delayed far into the night, they may have some food upon the appearance of the stars, but they must abstain from drinking intoxicating beverages.

On the day of their wedding, the bride and the bridegroom must make confession and with a contrite heart repent of their sins, and beseech God to grant them pardon, forgiveness and atonement. They should firmly resolve to devote themselves truly and sincerely to the worship of God. When they enter the nuptial canopy, they should pray that the Holy One cause His Divine Presence to rest among them.

The following is an appropriate prayer for a bride to be offered before her wedding:

"Almighty God, I pour out my heart in thanksgiving for the new joy that has come to ennoble my soul. O make me worthy of Thy gift and of the loving devotion of him whom Thy providence gives me as the companion of my life. Oh, how my heart throbs, how it pulsates between fear and hope! For I know the importance and the solemnity of this moment; I know that thenceforth my life will assume another form, that I take upon myself new, sacred duties, which are often so difficult to fulfill. Therefore, I pray unto Thee, O Lord: Do Thou assist me! Be Thou my guide, my shield and protector upon all my ways. Grant that I may remain united with my companion of life in unceasing fidelity and undisturbed harmony. Do Thou direct all our destinies into blessing, and guard us against all trials and tribulations.

"O Lord, strengthen me to be unto him a good and faithful wife. Fill me with the spirit of the faithful daughters of Israel, whose virtues have caused the hearts of their husbands safely to trust in them to the end of their days. Consecrate my heart wholly unto Thy service, and let me walk before Thee robed in purity. My home and hearth to Thee I devote; to Thee, and to all that is good and noble. May I realize how false is grace, how vain is beauty; and that she alone is blessed whom the Lord leads to acts of kindness and deeds of mercy.

"Merciful Father, forgive now, I entreat Thee, the follies of my years gone by, and the faults I have been guilty of against my beloved parents, elders, relations, and friends. Guard my new home from every form of disaster and misfortune; let many happy years be spent there, of love and peace and harmony, free from the envy of the lot of others, and free from the bane of others' envy. Bless and prosper the handiwork of our hands, and enable us to develop those noble traits of character which are the foundation of a true Jewish home. AMEN."

It is customary for the orphaned bride or bridegroom to give some charity on the day of the wedding, to visit the grave of the departed father or mother, and to offer a prayer.

A BRIDE'S PRAYER AT HER FATHER'S GRAVE

"Peace be to your spirit, dear father! Well do I know that you safely rest under the shadow of the Almighty. And yet to think that you are no more with me on earth, grieves the heart and saddens the thought. You have so lovingly cared for me; you have so long supported me, have watched over me, and you have anxiously awaited the time when I should be united with the beloved one of my heart. But it was the will of the Almighty that you be taken away from me before this happy day of my life. O how happy I would be to have you with me on this day of my union with my beloved, but the ways of the Lord must not be questioned.

"I have come to the place where the earthly part of you has been laid to rest, and at your grave I pray to Him, who has revealed Himself to us as a Father, that He grant that I remain united with my companion of life in unceasing fidelity and undisturbed harmony. I fervently pray to Him to direct all our destinies to blessings; to guard us against all trials and tribulations; to strengthen me to be unto my beloved a good and faithful wife, and to strengthen my beloved to be a good and faithful husband to me; to bless the days of our united life with peace and happiness. O Lord, grant that we may lead a pure and virtuous life, and that our union may be a rich source of virtue and pious joy.

"Dear father, I now pray in humble and filial love that you forgive whatever anxiety or worry I might have caused you when you were with me on earth, and whatever dishonor I might have caused you when you dwelt in the realm of the holy spirits. Forgive the acts of thoughtlessness and my lack of consideration for your wishes, so that I may enter under the nuptial canopy with the knowledge that your spirit will look down graciously upon me and my union. May the glory of God be upon you, beloved father, and His peace surround you, peace without end.

"Merciful Father in heaven, do not leave me nor forsake me, for thus it is written: 'Though father and mother forsake me, but Thou, O Lord, wilt take me up.' O bless our union. Amen."

[304]

A BRIDE'S PRAYER AT HER MOTHER'S GRAVE

"My dear beloved mother, for ever laid at rest in the lap of the earth. Your child draws nigh to you, on this solemn day of her life, with the tears of mourning in her eyes. Your spirit sojourns upon the heights of eternal light, but could you ever forget your child, still walking in the shadows of the earth? No, a mother's love is everlasting, eternal, even as her soul is eternal, even as God is eternal who implanted that love in her heart. In pain you gave me life, and yet you did greet me with a gladsome smile when I lay in your arms. Thus did you ever endure the sufferings of life and accept them with a mother's smile. Your first and your last glance at me was full of self sacrificing love. O sacred spirit of my mother, behold the tears flowing forth from the eye of your child in the memory of you; they are all that I can offer unto you; accept them, pray, as a sacrifice of thanks and love.

"Dearly beloved mother! On this day I am going to enter under the nuptial canopy with my beloved, and I feel your presence by the warm stream of feeling flowing through my soul at this moment. Yes, you still bear with me all my griefs, and you rejoice in my joys and happiness. I am very happy now, dear mother, when I am about to join my beloved in the sacred union of matrimony, and I know that your spirit will be present on this joyous occasion, and give me your motherly blessing.

"You, dear mother, taught my lips to utter the first word of prayer and direct your child's emotions towards God. You implanted pious thoughts in the heart of your child. Now, when I am to enter the bond of matrimony with my beloved, I pray at your grave for mercy and guidance from our Father in heaven, the Father of orphans. I pray to Him that He grant that I honor your precepts throughout my married life, though your lips are closed forever. I beseech the Lord that He strengthen my resolution that I forever be a true, faithful, and devoted wife to my beloved; and that my beloved be a faithful and devoted husband to me. May the Almighty bless our union with everlasting peace and contentment, and may sorrow and grief never enter our abode.

"O Lord God, may the love and faithfulness of my departed mother that guarded and guided me in my childhood, be forever written upon the tablet of my heart and set up as a memorial before my eyes, that I may ever find grace and favor in Thy sight, O Lord, and in the eyes of men. May my house become a shrine of virtue and good deeds.

"Eternal Father in heaven! bestow Thy peace on this consecrated grave, that the honored remains of my beloved mother may rest therein undisturbed. Vouchsafe an eternal abode of bliss to her glorified soul that she may find rest under the shadow of Thy wing. AMEN."

CHAPTER TEN

DEATH AND MOURNING

"Without thy consent wast thou created, and born into the world without any choice; thou art now living without thy volition, and wilt have to die without thy approval; so likewise without thy consent wilt thou have to render account before the Holy One, praised be He." (ABOT iv. 29).

NOTA KOSLOWSKY

CHAPTER TEN

DEATH AND MOURNING

LIFE AND DEATH The Jewish religion conceives of life on earth merely as a preparatory period for the life to come in the hereafter. The human lifetime is vain unless it is utilized for the purpose of accumulating good deeds, the reward for which will be reaped in the world to come. In the words of our great sages: "This world is like an antechamber before the world to come; prepare thyself in the antechamber that thou mayest be admitted into the reception hall."

According to Judaism, life is no mere empty struggle or dream that ends with death. Human beings do not exist and perish like cattle. They have a soul, a very portion of the throne of the Almighty, which was sent down from heaven to dwell in the body that it may perform the will of the Almighty, and then receive its reward in a world of everlasting bliss.

Death, as the Jew conceives of it, does not terminate life. Only the material body returns to dust, but the soul, which is a portion from God, returns to heaven when it rids itself of the body. For the soul life begins anew, after the body's death, in the world to come. There people receive their rewards or punishments in accordance with their merits and their deeds during the body's span of life on earth.

Life is therefore a sacred thing, and must not be spent merely in bodily pleasures, but must be devoted chiefly to carrying out the will of the Almighty. Death, according to this conception, is really the ultimate goal of life, when the soul, freed from its material encasement, becomes pure and holy, soaring to its origin in the high heavens. Death is therefore more sacred than life.

In recognition of the holiness of life, the Jew must perform every deed in sanctity. Every act must be done for the sake of Him who gave us life. To show that death is the holy goal of a sacred life, the Jew, from time immemorial, laid down many rules of law concerning the dying person, the treatment of the dead, and mourning. It is the sacred duty of every Jew to become acquainted with these laws.

CONFESSION BEFORE DEATH According to our great Talmudic sages, all those who make confession of their sins before their death have a share in the world to come. Therefore, when a man or a woman is gravely sick, he or she should make confession. And let not any one fear that evil will ensue because of the confession, for many were they who have confessed and become well again, and there were also many who neglected to confess and died. On the contrary, as a reward for making confession, one's life will be prolonged and a cure granted.

If the invalid is unable to confess by word of mouth, she should make a mental confession; and if she is able to speak but little, she should say this very short confession: "May my death be an atonement for all my sins."

A brief form of confession is as follows:

"O my God and God of my fathers! Let my prayer come before Thee, and disregard not my supplication. O forgive all the sins I have committed from my birth until this day. I am abashed of my evil deeds and transgressions. Pray accept my pain and suffering as an expiation, and forgive my wrong-doing, for against Thee alone have I sinned.

"May it be Thy will, O my God and God of my fathers, that I sin no more; and purge the sins I have committed with full mercy, not by means of affliction and disease. O send for me, and for all sick persons in Israel, a perfect cure and healing.

"I acknowledge unto Thee, O my God and God of my fathers, that both my cure and death depend on Thy will. May it be Thy will to heal me. Yet if Thou hast decreed that I shall die of this disease, may my death expiate for all my sins, iniquities, and transgressions which I have committed before Thee. Grant me shelter in the shadow of Thy wings and a portion in Gan Eden, which is reserved for the righteous.

"Father of the orphan and Judge of the widow, protect my beloved kindred, with whose soul my soul is bound up.

"Into Thy hand I commit my spirit; Thou hast redeemed me, O Lord God of truth.

"Hear O Israel, the Lord our God, the Lord is one.

"The Lord He is God. The Lord He is God."

If the invalid desires to make a lengthy confession, she may adopt the one recited on the Day of Atonement.

WHEN A PERSON IS DYING Life, as a precious gift given by God, cannot and may not be taken away by a human being. It is therefore a serious crime in the Jewish law for a person to commit suicide or to take the life of others. Only the Almighty, the Giver of life, can take His gift back and deprive a living being of life. Nothing should therefore be done to accelerate death. For this reason, we are forbidden to touch or move the body of a dying person, lest his death be hastened.

Even if the patient is suffering a painful and slow death, and is causing great suffering to the patient's kindred, it is nevertheless forbidden to hasten, even in an indirect manner, the patient's death.

From the moment a person is in the grip of death, she must not be left alone to die. Those present at the time of the soul's departure should be extremely careful not to engage in idle or frivolous conversation.

It is forbidden to do anything in connection with the funeral before life has departed.

It is forbidden to partake of any food in the room where the deceased lies, unless a partition is erected. Even eating fruit or drinking water is forbidden. It is likewise forbidden to pronounce any benediction there.

The corpse should not be handled on the Sabbath, even if it is for the purpose of performing some religious duty.

ACCOMPANYING THE DEAD Our Talmudic sages included the precept of "accompanying the dead to their rest" among the ten for the fulfillment of which "the fruit is reaped in this world, whilst its principal is laid up for the world to come."

It is the duty of every man and woman to accompany the dead during the funeral procession for a distance of at least four cubits (about six feet). One who sees a coffin pass by and fails to join the procession is likened to one who mocks and sneers at the poor, and deserves to be excommunicated.

THE RENDING OF THE GARMENTS It was an ancient custom among the Hebrews to rend their garments as a sign of grief upon receiving bad news. Jacob, for instance, tore his garments when he learned that the coat of his beloved son Joseph had been found torn and stained with blood.

It is therefore customary to make a rent in one's garments for the loss of one's next of kin for whom one is required to observe mourning. (See "Seven Days of Mourning" page 325). This ceremony must be performed while standing; if it is performed while the mourner is seated, the obligation is not fulfilled, and it must be repeated in the proper fashion. It is best to tear the clothes when one's sorrow is still intense before the coffin is closed.

Unless the deceased is one's father or mother, one need not make a rent every time one changes one's garments during the seven days of mourning.

Every mourner should honor the Sabbath by wearing other clothes, but not those garments especially set aside for the Sabbath. If the mourner has no other weekday clothes than those that contain the sign of mourning, the mourner must turn the rent inside, so that it is invisible, because public mourning is forbidden on the Sabbath.

Unless the deceased is one's father or mother, the rent may be basted together after the seven days of mourning, and completely sewed up after the thirty days. In the case of mourning for a father or a mother, the rent may be basted after thirty days and never completely sewed up.

AN ONAN Any woman who loses by death one of her next kin for whom she is bound to observe mourning (see page 325), is termed *onan* from the time of the death until after the interment.

An *onan* is exempt from observing all precepts, because of the honor due the dead. However, she must observe all the prohibitory laws.

An *onan* is not permitted to have sexual intercourse, bathe, anoint herself with oil, eat meat, drink wine, participate in joyous celebrations, greet friends, partake of an elaborate meal, powder herself, sit on a chair, sleep in bed, or do any work for profit.

As a sign of mourning, the mourner may not remove her shoes before the interment takes place. She is permitted to leave the house if need be to make provisions for the burial.

If death occurs on the Sabbath, on which day the law prohibits burying the dead, the mourner is not subject to the laws relating to an *onan*. She is permitted to partake of meat and wine, and is obliged to observe all precepts, but she is not permitted to have sexual intercourse.

THE SHROUDS A human being, made in the image of God, deserves respect even when the body is dead. The corpse must be prepared for burial in accordance with the time-honored customs of the Jewish people. The women who prepare the shrouds and wash the body of a dead person must be familiar with these laws and customs.

It is forbidden to begin preparing the shrouds before life has departed.

It is customary to make the shrouds of fine white linen, but they must not be too costly.

Neither a hem or a knot of any sort may be made while sewing the shrouds, or when dressing the dead.

The shrouds should consist of no less than three garments: the shirt, the breeches, and the overgarment with a girdle. White stockings should be put on the legs of the corpse, and a white cap on the head. An additional overgarment should be placed on the shoulders.

THE PURIFICATION OF THE BODY The rite of washing the body before burial, should not be commenced before the shrouds are ready.

The body of a dead girl or woman must be attended only by persons of the same sex.

During the washing of the body, the same respect must be shown as to the living. No idle conversation should be indulged in, but it is permissible to speak of the necessary preparations for the funeral. If the body must be moved from one place to another, it must be done by at least two persons, to prevent the corpse's legs and hands from being suspended.

Those engaged in attending the dead, shall say the following prayer before commencing their duties:

"O kind and merciful Lord God! Thy ways are truthful and benevolent, and Thou hast commanded us to deal kindly and benevolently with the dead by attending to their burial. May it, therefore, be Thy will, O Lord God, to strengthen and encourage us in performing this holy task of cleansing and washing the body, of putting on the shrouds, and of burying the dead. Mayest Thou keep us from all harm and injury, and may the work of our hands be faultless, in accordance with what is written: 'He who observes the Law shall experience no evil.' May the merit of performing this act of loving-kindness obtain for us the reward of completing the days of our life in welfare; and may the kindness of the Lord God ever rest on us. AMEN."

The entire body, including the head, should be washed with warm water. The fingers and toes, as well as all other parts of the body, should be thoroughly cleansed. The hair should be combed.

The corpse must be entirely enveloped in a white sheet while being cleansed, and the body should be washed while half covered, by holding up the ends of the sheet. The washing must be started from the head, and then downward to the feet.

Care should be taken not to place the body with its face downward, as that is a degrading position, but it should be inclined, first on one side, then on the other.

After the body has been thoroughly cleansed, it should be placed in a standing position, and about twenty-four quarts of water should be poured over the head so that it runs down the entire body. This last operation constitutes the real purification. While the water is poured over the corpse, the mouth should be covered by hand or otherwise, to prevent the water from running into it. The body is then thoroughly dried.

When pouring the water on the corpse, it is customary to recite the following: "And I will pour upon you pure water, and ye shall be cleansed; from all your uncleanliness and abominations will I purify you."

It is not necessary that the twenty-four

quarts of water be poured out of one vessel as two or even three vessels (but no more than three) may be combined to make up the required quantity. It is, however, necessary to commence pouring out the contents of the second vessel before the first is finished. Even when pouring the water out of one vessel, the flow must not be interrupted.

Then an egg is beaten with a little wire (the beating should be done in the shell of the egg), and the head of the dead washed therewith.

Care should be taken not to allow the fingers of the dead person's hand to remain closed.

The board upon which the corpse has been washed must not be turned over.

THE OBJECTS TO BE BURIED WITH BODY It is forbidden to derive any benefit from either the dead body or from the shrouds, whether it be of a Jew or non-Jew. Ornamental objects which are attached to the corpse, as for instance, a wig tied to, or woven into the hair, or artificial teeth, must be interred with the body. Jewelry, clothes, and all other objects not attached to the body, may, of course, be used by the living.

THE MEAL OF CONDOLENCE The first meal on the first day of mourning, must not consist of the mourner's own food. It is therefore a religious duty devolving upon the mourner's neighbors to supply the food for the first meal, which is known as the "Meal of Condolence." The reason for this rule of law is obvious. A woman in dire distress is in need of friendly neighbors and their consolation.

If the mourner's first meal after burial is delayed until nightfall, it may, inasmuch as the first day has passed, be then made of the mourner's own food. A mourner living a lone life without neighbors to contribute food for the meal of condolence, should therefore fast until nightfall; nevertheless, a woman unable to fast, is not obliged to suffer, but is allowed to eat of her own food.

To women in mourning, the meal of condolence should be supplied by women and not by men.

If the burial has taken place at night and the mourner desires to eat during that night, she is forbidden to eat of her own food, but she should be provided with food for the meal of condolence. Should she not desire to eat during that night, she is forbidden to eat the first meal of her own food the following day, since the first day of mourning is not over until sunset.

If the burial takes place on a Friday after three o'clock in the afternoon, the mourner should not be served with a meal of condolence in deference to the Sabbath. The mourner should abstain from eating anything until the evening.

If the burial takes place on a Festival, the meal of condolence is not served to the mourner; but if it takes place on the Intermediate Days of a Festival, a meal of condolence should be served.

A married woman is not allowed to take the first meal of her husband's food, for inasmuch as it devolves upon him to support her, it is considered as her own food.

PERIOD OF MOURNING Our sages have divided the period of mourning, in accordance with the biblical law, into three stages of varying intensity. The first period, known as *shibeah* (seven), refers to the first seven days of mourning. The laws pertaining to these seven days are most stringent. The second period, known as *sheloshim* (thirty), relates to the first thirty days after a death. The third period embraces the twelve months from the time a death occurs.

The Jewish law distinguishes between mourning to be observed for one's parent and that to be observed for all other next of kin. In the former case, the laws and regulations of mourning are much more severe.

THE SEVEN DAYS OF MOURNING (SHIBEAH) One is obliged to observe the rite of mourning on the death of the following next of kin: one's father; mother; son; daughter; brother, or sister, whether from father's side or mother's side; wife or husband.

For the death of a child that did not live thirty full days, the rite of mourning need not be observed.

The period of mourning begins as soon as the dead is buried and the grave is filled with earth.

During the first three days of mourning, the mourner should neither greet nor be greeted by any one. If others, through ignorance, offer a greeting, the mourner is not allowed to respond to their greetings but should inform them that he or she is a mourner. After the third day and until the seventh, the mourner must not greet others, but may respond to the uncalled for greetings of others.

During one's seven days of mourning, one

may not have sexual intercourse, wear leather footwear, leave one's house unless on matters of great urgency, and sit on chairs instead of the prescribed low bench or stool. One may walk about or stand, but must be seated when others offer condolences. One is not permitted to laugh or rejoice. One may wash only one's hands, face, and feet, and these only in cold water. Bathing, anointing, and massaging are permissible for medicinal or hygienic purposes only. The wearing of a freshly washed garment, even a shirt, is forbidden, even if it is in honor of the Sabbath.

A mourner may not perform any work, except such housework as is actually necessary, during the seven days of mourning.

On the Sabbath that occurs during the seven days of mourning, all the rules regulating the mourner's private life must be observed, such as the prohibition against sexual intercourse and bathing. No rites of mourning, however, are to be observed in public.

The Sabbath day is included in the total of the first seven days of mourning.

A candle or a lamp should be kept burning for the departed soul during the seven days of mourning, especially when the prayers are offered.

During one's first thirty days of **THE THIRTY** mourning, one is forbidden to **wear** **DAYS** Sabbath clothes even on the Sab- **(SHELOSHIM)** bath. One is forbidden, of course, **AND THE** **TWELVE** to put on new clothes. One who **MONTHS** mourns for a parent is forbidden, according to custom, to put on new clothes during the entire year. If, however, one is compelled to buy new clothes, one should not put them on until another has first worn them for two or three days.

One is forbidden during the first thirty days of mourning for one's next of kin, and during the first twelve months of mourning the death of a parent, to join in any celebration, even of a religious duty, such as a circumcision, the redemption of first-born, or a wedding. The mourner may, however, participate in a religious feast celebrated at the mourner's house, provided it is not a wedding feast.

During the first thirty days of mourning for one's next of kin, and the twelve months of mourning for one's parent, one is not permitted either to send or receive gifts, or to enter a house where a wedding feast is being celebrated. After the first thirty days, however, the mourner may act as bride's maid in escorting the bride under the nuptial canopy, and on that occasion may put on Sabbath clothes.

A mourner is permitted to serve as waitress at a wedding, and may in her own house eat whatever is sent her from the feast.

It is customary for a mourner to change her place at the synagogue during the first thirty days of mourning for her next of kin, and during the first twelve months of mourning for her parent. The new place should be at least four cubits (about six feet) distant from her accustomed seat and further removed from the Holy Ark.

EXCESSIVE GRIEF IS FORBIDDEN It is strictly forbidden to grieve excessively over the dead. We must acknowledge that the Lord God is righteous in all His ways. "The Lord gave and the Lord took, may the name of the Lord be blessed," said Job in his great grief, when told that he had lost all his sons and daughters. Our great Talmudic scholars write that the Holy One says: "You are not permitted to be more compassionate than I am." Therefore, one should not weep or mourn excessively over the dead.

A very interesting story is recorded in the

Bible which illustrates the necessity of abstaining from excessive mourning.

The son that Bath-sheba had born to King David was stricken with a serious illness. For six days and nights King David prayed to God, and refused to eat bread together with the royal family. He spent his nights sleeping upon the ground. The elders vainly pleaded with the king to moderate his grief.

On the seventh day, the child died, and the members of the royal family feared to inform the king of the child's death; they said: "While the child was yet alive, the king prayed, fasted, and slept on the ground; now, if we tell him that the child is dead, he may do himself some harm."

But when David observed that his servants whispered together, he surmised that the child was dead, and he inquired of them: "Is the child dead?" And they replied: "He is dead."

Thereupon King David arose from the ground, washed and anointed himself, changed his apparel, and went to the house of the Lord and worshiped. He then came back to his palace, and requested that food be set before him, and he began to eat. His servants asked in amazement: "While the child was alive, you fasted and wept for him, but when the child was dead, you arose and ate bread?"

The king, in his implicit faith in God, responded: "While the child was yet alive, I fasted and wept, for I thought the Lord might be gracious to me and spare the child's life. But now he is dead, why should I fast? Can I bring him back again? I shall go to him, but he will not return to me."

JAHRZEIT (ANNIVERSARY) OF DEATH) It is the religious duty of every person to observe the anniversary of the death of one's father or mother, by fasting, in order that one may be impelled to repentance, and self-criticism. By doing this, one obtains Divine grace for one's father or mother who will be elevated in Paradise.

It is customary to kindle a light on the eve of the *jahrzeit*, which is kept burning for twenty-four hours. This practice is linked with the thought expressed by King Solomon: "The spirit of man is the lamp of the Lord."

If one is not certain of the date of one's parent's death, one should select the approximate date, and should always observe that day as the *jahrzeit*.

The following is an appropriate prayer to

be offered on the anniversary of one's parent's
death:

"O Lord and merciful Father, Thou art
everlasting, but we are strangers and sojourners
on this earth, as were our fathers before us. All
that remains of us on earth is the memory of
our deeds, cherished by loving hearts, whilst
our soul returns to God, its everlasting source.
Humbly and devoutly, therefore, do I pray for
the peace of my beloved father (mother), whose
mortal part is imbedded in the bosom of the
earth.

"I recall, on this day of saddest recollec-
tions, with greater vividness than on all other
days, the blessed memory of my departed father
(mother). With fervent gratitude do I remember how great a comfort didst thou, O God,
grant to me, as long as my well-beloved was
with me. If I have been unmindful of Thy
goodness while it was my portion in life, I now
deeply regret my forgetfulness and humbly beseech Thy forgiveness.

"O God, teach me the true value of this
day, that more of Thy wisdom may enter my
heart. Help me to feel that my dear father
(mother) is in Thy peaceful keeping.

"My dear father (mother) is gone; but all
the goodness, the sweetness and nobility of that

life I well remember. As this light burns pure
and clear, so may the blessed memory of the
goodness, the nobility of character of my dear
father (mother) illumine my soul. May the
hallowed influence of this day give me strength
to do Thy will, O God, with a steadfast, sub-
missive and loving spirit. May the remembrance
of the life of my dear father (mother) be to
me an incentive to goodness, a shield against
temptation and passion, a source of comfort
and strength in all the vicissitudes of life.

"May the soul of my departed father
(mother) be bound up in life everlasting.
AMEN."

DEDICATION OF TOMBSTONE It is an ancient custom in Israel
to set up a tombstone at the head
of the grave in honor of the departed.

The prevailing custom is not to put up the
tombstone until twelve months after death.

The following prayer should be offered on
the occasion of dedicating a tombstone:

"All-kind and merciful Father, a thousand
years in Thy sight are but as yesterday, and the
years of our life are but a span.

"In Thine unsearchable wisdom, Thou hast taken our dear . . . from us. But the deep and tender love which attached us unto our . . . is strong as death. Striving to soothe the sorrow of our hearts, we dedicate this stone to-day.

"In consecrating it to the memory of the departed, may we at the same time dedicate unto the living the love with which our dear one filled our lives. So may we realize the truth of the sacred Writ: 'The memory of the righteous is a blessing.'

"Let us go hence with a deeper and broader love for life and humanity. Then shall we feel that the more nobly we live, the more sincere will be the tribute we shall pay our dead.

"In this spirit, O God, we offer our prayers to Thee. Fill our hearts with humility, that we may truly know that Thy thoughts are not our thoughts. Help us so to live that the purity and godliness of our lives may bring honor to the memory of the dear ones who dwell in peace with Thee. Thus shall we erect for them their truest, their lasting memorial among men.

"May the soul of our departed be bound up in life everlasting.

"Praised be. Thou, O God, who givest life and takest it away. AMEN."

MEMORIAL SERVICE

It is an established custom in Israel to memorialize the souls of the departed, to pray for them, and to contribute to charity for their sake. Prayers and charity are helpful to the departed.

The souls of the departed are memorialized four times during the year: on the last day of Passover, on the second day of Shabuot, on Shemini Atzeret (the eighth day of Sukkoth), and on Yom Kippur. On each occasion, charitable contributions are made in their behalf.

Those who have parents living usually leave the synagogue when the Memorial Services are read.

Before memorializing the dead, the following is recited:

"O Lord, what is man, that Thou takest knowledge of him; or the son of man, that Thou makest account of him! Man is like unto vanity; his days are as a shadow that passes away. In the morning he flourishes, and grows up; in the evening he is cut down and withers. So teach us to number our days, that we may achieve wisdom. Mark the perfect man, and behold the upright; for the end of that man is peace. But God will relieve my soul from the grasp of the grave; for He will receive me. My flesh and my heart fails; but God is the strength of my heart and my portion for ever. And the dust returns to the earth as it was, but the spirit returns to God who gave it. I shall behold Thy countenance in righteousness; I shall be satisfied when I awake, with Thy similtude."

In Memory of the Father

May God remember the soul of my revered father who has gone unto eternity, and in whose memory I now offer to contribute to charity. In reward of this, may his soul be bound up in the bond of eternal life, together with the souls of Abraham, Isaac, and Jacob, Sarah, Rebecca Rachel, and Leah, and all other righteous men and women that are in Paradise; and let us say: Amen.

Thy memory, dearly beloved father, this solemn hour fills my soul, revives in me all the holy sentiments of love and tenderness which you lavished so richly on me when you lived on earth. Your image will live for ever in my soul, as my guiding star on the path of virtue; and when my pilgrimage on earth is ended and

I shall arrive at the throne of mercy, may I
be deemed worthy of you in the presence of
God. May our merciful Father reward you for
the faithful kindness you have shown me; may
He grant you eternal peace! Amen.

O God, full of compassion, Thou who
dwellest on high! Grant perfect rest beneath
the sheltering wings of Thy presence, among
the holy and pure who shine as the brightness
of the firmament, unto the soul of my revered
father who has gone unto eternity, and in whose
memory I now offer to contribute to charity.
May his repose be in Paradise. May the Lord of
mercy bring him under the cover of His wings
for ever, and may his soul be bound up in the
bond of eternal life. May the Lord be his
possession, and may his repose be peace. Amen.

In Memory of the Mother

May God remember the soul of my revered
mother who has gone unto eternity, and in
whose memory I now offer to contribute to
charity. In reward of this, may her soul be
bound up in the bond of eternal life, together
with the souls of Abraham, Isaac, and Jacob,
Sarah, Rebecca, Rachel, and Leah, and all other
righteous men and women that are in Paradise;
and let us say: Amen.

I remember you in this solemn hour, dearly beloved mother. I remember the days when you still dwelt on earth, and your tender love watched over me like a guardian angel. You have gone from me, but the bond which unites our souls can never be severed; your image truly lives within my heart. May the merciful Father reward you for the faithful kindness you have ever shown me; may He lift up the light of His countenance in mercy upon you, and grant you eternal peace. Amen.

O God, full of compassion, Thou who dwellest on high! Grant perfect rest beneath the sheltering wings of Thy presence, among the holy and pure who shine as the brightness of the firmament, unto the soul of my revered mother who has gone unto eternity, and in whose memory I now offer to contribute to charity. May her repose be in Paradise. May the Lord of mercy bring her under the cover of His wings for ever, and may her soul be bound up in the bond of eternal life. May the Lord be her possession, and may her repose be peace. Amen.

In Memory of the Husband

(Recite the first prayer given for Memory of
the Father, Page 335, substituting the word
husband for **father,** and then add:)

I remember you in this solemn hour, you
dearly beloved friend of my youth. I remember the happy days we lived together; I remember the tender affection, the self denial
which filled your being while we still walked
hand in hand the common path of our wedded
life, and when your love and fidelity were my
comfort, and your counsel and aid my support.
Though death has summoned you from my side,
your image still lives in my heart, is still an
inspiration to me, and your spirit continues to
live in a higher existence. May God cover you
with the shadow of His grace, and give you
eternal peace. Amen.

(Continue with the third prayer given on
page 336 for Memory of Father, substituting
the word **husband** for **father.**)

In Memory of a Child

I remember you in this solemn hour, my
beloved child. I remember the days, when I
still delighted in your bloom, in your bodily
and mental growth, in beautiful hopes for your
future. The inscrutable will of God took you
early from me; He called you to His abode;

yet in my wounded heart the fond remembrance of you can never be extinguished. But the Almighty is kind and just in all His ways; His holy name may be praised forever. His paternal love is my solace, my staff and support, and on it I rest my hope for your eternal destiny. As a father pities his children, may He look with compassion upon you, and cause your portion ever to be a blissful one. Amen.

In Memory of Grandparents and Relatives

May God remember the souls of my grand-fathers and grandmothers, my uncles and my aunts, my brothers and my sisters, whether paternal or maternal, who have gone unto eternity, and in whose memory I now offer to contribute to charity. In reward of this, may their souls be bound up in the bond of eternal life, together with the souls of Abraham, Isaac, and Jacob, Sarah, Rebecca, Rachel, and Leah, and all righteous men and women who are in Paradise; and let us say: Amen.

At the conclusion of Memorial Service, the following prayer is read:

"Father of mercy, in whose hands are the souls of the living and the dead, may Thy consolation cheer us as we remember on this day our beloved and revered kinsfolk who have gone to their rest. May their souls repose in the land of eternal life, beholding Thy glory and delighting in Thy goodness.

"And now, O good and beneficent God, what shall we say, and what shall we speak unto Thee? Our needs are many, our knowledge slender. Shame covers us as often as the remembrances of all Thy love for us rises within our minds. O turn this day in lovingkindness and tender mercy to the prayers of Thy servants who pour out their souls before Thee. May Thy lovingkindness not depart from us. Give us our needful sustenance, and let us not be in want of the gifts of flesh and blood. Remove from us all worry and grief, distress and fear, shame and contempt. Let Thy grace be with us, that we may ever rear our children to keep Thy commandments and to fulfill Thy will all the days of their life.

"O God, take us not hence in the midst of our days. Let us complete in peace the number of our years. Help us, O God of our salvation, to bear ourselves faithfully and blamelessly during the years of our pilgrimage. Amen and Amen."

YIZKOR CALENDAR

Year	8th Day of Passover	Second Day of Shavuoth	Day of Atonement	Shemini Atsereth
1973	April 24	June 7	Oct. 6	Oct. 18
1974	April 14	May 28	Sept. 26	Oct. 8
1975	April 3	May 17	Sept. 15	Sept. 27
1976	April 22	June 5	Oct. 4	Oct. 16
1977	April 10	May 24	Sept. 22	Oct. 4
1978	April 29	June 12	Oct. 11	Oct. 23
1979	April 19	June 2	Oct. 1	Oct. 13
1980	April 8	May 22	Sept. 20	Oct. 2
1981	April 26	June 9	Oct. 8	Oct. 20
1982	April 15	May 29	Sept. 27	Oct. 9
1983	April 5	May 19	Sept. 17	Sept. 29
1984	April 24	June 7	Oct. 6	Oct. 18
1985	April 13	May 27	Sept. 25	Oct. 7
1986	May 1	June 14	Oct. 13	Oct. 25
1987	April 21	June 4	Oct. 3	Oct. 15
1988	April 9	May 23	Sept. 21	Oct. 3
1989	April 27	June 10	Oct. 9	Oct. 21
1990	April 17	May 31	Sept. 29	Oct. 11
1991	April 6	May 20	Sept. 18	Sept. 30
1992	April 25	June 8	Oct. 7	Oct. 19

INDEX

A

AB, ninth of, 257, 258
ABRAHAM, founder of the Jewish religion, 20; visited by the Almighty when sick, 38; taught greatness of hospitality, 41; listened to Sarah's advice, 273.
ACTIONS, see *Deeds.*
ADAM, allowed to eat only vegetables, 87.
ADULTERY, punishment for, 269.
AGRICULTURAL FESTIVALS, 148, 168, 182.
AHASUERUS, agreed to destroy all Jews, 233.
AHIMELECH, the priest, 58.
AKIBA, his daughter saved from death, 33; supporter of revolution against Rome, 246.
ALKABIZ, author of *Lekah Dodi*, 119.
ALMIGHTY, to adopt His attributes, 38-39.
ALMS, how to be given, 37.
ANGELS, accompanying men on Sabbath eve, 130.
ANGER, a grave vice, 66.
ANIMALS, to rest on Sabbath, 51; must be pitied even when belonging to enemy, 52; unnecessary pain to, forbidden 52; must be fed first, 53; forbidden as food, 81, 87, 91.
APOSTEMUS, burned the Torah, 257.
ARBOR DAY, 252.
ARROGANCE, an extreme vice 65.
ATONEMENT, Day of, see *Yom Kippur.*

B

BABYLONIA, Jews in, informed of the New Moon, 250.
BABYLONIAN RABBIS, told not to drop extra festival day, 140.
BACON, see *hog meat.*

BARAK, a warrior of the tribe of Naphtali, 25.
BAR KOKHBA, revolution of, 245, 258.
BAR MITZVAH, definition of, 281.
BENEDICTION, on affixing *mezuzah*, 76; one suffices for many *mezuzot*, 76; on washing hands in the morning, 77; on putting on the fringed garment (*arba kanfot*), 79; over hand-washing before meals, 84; over bread, 84; over fruit growing on trees, 85; over fruit growing on ground, 86; over food other than bread prepared from wheat, etc., 86; before drinking wine, 86; before eating dairy, or fish, or drinking any beverage other than wine, 87; upon immersing vessels 107; when separating *hallah*, 109; must be said immediately before performance of precept, 126; over Sabbath candles, 127; on the *erub tabshilin* ceremony, 144; on search for leaven, 152; before eating *matzah*, 156; over candles on first two days of Passover, 162; over candles on last two days of Passover, 166; over candles on Shabuot, 173; when sitting in the *sukkah*, 178; upon lighting candles on first two days of *Sukkot*, 179; over the four species, 183; over candles on *Shemini Atzeret*, 186; over candles on *Simhat Torah*, 188; over the *Rosh Hashanah* candles, 195; over *Yom Kippur* candles, 209; over *Hanukkah* candles, 226; when immersing, 298; not to be pronounced in presence of dead person, 315.
BETHAR, city of, conquered by Romans, 257.
BET-YAZEK, court of, 259.

[343]

INDEX

INDEX

295; ritual bath of, 296; on the close of Sabbath or festival, 296.

INFORMER, what constitutes, 64.

INJURIES, to persons, 64.

INSULT, forbidden, 66-67.

INTERMARRIAGE, forbidden, 283.

INTESTINES, examination of, 91, 100.

ISAAC, destined to carry on Jewish faith, 273.

ISAIAH, reproaches Jews, 259; comforts his people, 263.

ISHMAEL, the inheritor of a pagan culture, 273.

ISRAELITES, decreed to die in the wilderness, 257.

J

JABIN, a Canaanitish king, 24.

JACOB, tore garments in grief, 316.

JAEL, killed Sisera, 25-26.

JAHRZEIT, 330; light lit on day of, 330; prayer for day of, 331.

JEALOUSY, leads to commission of crime, 62; a grave vice, 67.

JEPHTAH, his rash vow, 48-49; his daughter's devotion, 48.

JERUSALEM, ploughed over, 257.

JEW, not to be selfish, 141, 221.

JEWISH COAT OF MAIL, 78.

JEWISH HOMELAND, never forgotten by Jew, 23; see also Palestine.

JEWISH PEOPLE, origin of, 20; called a 'kingdom of priests,' 72.

JEWISH RELIGION, cardinal principle of, 21; embraces every phase of life, 72.

JEWS, martyrs of barbaric intolerance, 19; first to introduce morality, tolerance, peace, 23; in Canaan under tribal system, 24; must follow ways of the Almighty, 38-39; miracle of their existence, 221.

JOSEPH, Rab, 123.

JOSEPH, the honorer of Sabbath, 120.

JUDAH HANASI, his attitude toward animals, 43.

JUDGMENT, not to invoke judgment of, 66.

K

KAPPAROT, custom of, 205.

KASHERING UTENSILS, for the Passover, 150.

KEREN KAYYEMET, 172. ....

KIDDUSH, over wine, 131; over hallot, 131; where to be made, 131; on festivals, 142; on Passover, 163.

KITCHEN UTENSILS, two sets of, 104.

"KNOCK ON WOOD," a foolish superstition, 57.

KOL NIDRE, service of, 214.

KOSHER FOOD, reason for using, 88-89; duty of woman to supply her home with, 89.

KOSHER MEAT, what constitutes, 90-91.

KREPLACH, on Hoshanah Rabbah, 185; before Yom Kippur, 207; on Purim, 236, 241.

L

LAG BAOMER, meaning of, 245; a school children's holiday, 247.

LAMENTATIONS, 259, 260, 261.

LATKES, on Hanukkah, 222.

LAUGHTER, day of, see Purim.

LAW, study of, 30; basic principle of, 31.

LEGS, how salted, 102.

LEKAH DODI, poem of, 119.

LEAVENED FOOD, search for, 150; formula after search of, 152; when eaten on day before Passover, 157; at conclusion of Passover, 167. (See hametz).

LIARS, punishment of, 67.

LIES, see untruths.

LIFE, in concept of Jewish re'

N

INDEX